More Praise for Je...

Dreams a...

"This book is written with love, interest and conviction. Jeanne's aim is to teach us the importance of dreams for those in contact with the dying and the people closest to them. Easy to read and understand. Do not hesitate to seize this opportunity in discovering another tool for accompaniment."

—Monique Séguin, co-author of *Dreams and Death*

"Grief counselor Van Bronkhorst... concentrates on using dreams to help give new insights and relate to others for the dying and those close to them. She maintains that dreams can assist people to focus on what's important, mourn alongside others, and be close with those who are gone. The author details how to listen to and open conversations with one's dreams, as they offer a way to talk about the imminent death in a nonthreatening way... superb in discussing preparation for death."

—*Library Journal* (starred review)

Praise for *Premonitions in Daily Life*

"*Premonitions in Daily Life* is a superb look at a very common experience—the sense of knowing a future event... Van Bronkhorst takes the mystery and confusion out of premonitions with this fascinating, reader-friendly book."

—Larry Dossey, MD, author of *The Power of Premonitions*

"[Van Bronkhorst] has compiled an in-depth series of guidelines for how to identify premonitions, how to normalize them, and how to integrate them in a sensible and useful way into your life."

—Sally Rhine Feather PhD, author of *The Gift*

dreams

——— *at the* ———

threshold

About the Author

Jeanne Van Bronkhorst has worked with people facing life-threatening illness for twenty years, including ten years as a hospice social worker and bereavement counselor. She has led grief groups and trained volunteers in how to sit with grief for several different hospice organizations in the United States and Canada. She has graduate degrees in psychology and in social work and a strong interest in social science research. She began writing full time several years ago and her first book, *Premonitions in Daily Life: Working With Spontaneous Information When Rational Understanding Fails You* (2013), has been translated into three languages. Her lifelong interest in dreams led her to introduce dream appreciation into her hospice work, which proved so useful a tool it became the origin for this book. She lives in Toronto and is now working on a research project with healthcare professionals in Canada and the United States about patient dreams.

Guidance, Comfort, and Healing at the End of Life

dreams

—— *at the* ——

threshold

Jeanne Van Bronkhorst

Llewellyn Publications
Woodbury, Minnesota

FIRST EDITION
First Printing, 2015

Cover art: Shutterstock/183854153/©Helen Hotson
Cover design: Kevin R. Brown
Editing: Stephanie Finne

For credit information for previously published works, please see pages 259–260.

Llewellyn Publications is a registered trademark of Llewellyn Worldwide Ltd.

Library of Congress Cataloging-in-Publication Data
Van Bronkhorst, Jeanne, 1962–
    Dreams at the threshold : guidance, comfort, and healing at the end of life / by Jeanne Van Bronkhorst. — First edition.
        pages   cm
    Includes bibliographical references and index.
    ISBN 978-0-7387-4234-2
    1. Death—Psychological aspects. 2. Dreams—Psychological aspects. 3. Terminally ill--Care. I. Title.
    BF789.D4V36 2015
    154.6'3—dc23
                            2014035916

Llewellyn Publications
A Division of Llewellyn Worldwide Ltd.
2143 Wooddale Drive
Woodbury, MN 55125-2989
www.llewellyn.com

Printed in the United States of America

Also by Jeanne Van Bronkhorst

Premonitions in Daily Life

*For Ann Malain, who has given me a life of joy and belonging,
and for all the dreams we carry in our hearts.*

Contents

Epilogue: Dreams of Purpose and Meaning . . . 249

Reprinted Materials . . . 259

Acknowledgments

I am so grateful to Susan Simmons for her editing and coaching. Through our weekly phone meetings she has held my hand, laughed at my jokes, asked pointed questions, and generally helped push my ideas through the agony of development into a final polished product. She is my first and last reader and a good friend, and I feel incredibly lucky to have met her.

Angela Wix at Llewellyn Publications is a warm and generous presence who has now championed two of my books through the publication process. I am grateful for her work and the work of the many Llewellyn staff, especially Nanette Stearns, Editorial Director; Katie Mickschl; and Stephanie Finne, who helped ready this book for publication. There is an extraordinary amount of work involved in getting a book ready for print, and I am grateful you included me in so many steps along the way.

I am indebted to all the people who agreed to be interviewed. Your experiences, both professional and personal, form the backbone of this book. Alice Priestly, Catherine (Kit) Martin, Christopher Sowton, Craig Knorr, Fiona Martins, Gail

Tyson, Jay Libby, Judy Callahan, Katherine Rose, Kathy Flores, Mary Van Bronkhorst, Michele Chaban, Monique Seguin, Peggy Zammit, Phyllis Russell, Susan McCoy, Susan Simmons, Tallulah Lyons, and Tony Cheung. Many thanks as well to the research team at the Center for Hospice and Palliative Care in Buffalo, New York: Pei Grant, Christopher Kerr, Scott Wright, and Rachel Depner. Your groundbreaking work is going to help many people.

I am grateful to the many clients and families I have met who've shown me how grace and healing at the end of life is possible. They have enriched my view of the world and given many lessons in the importance of appreciating life in the moment. I am also grateful to my colleagues—social workers, nurses, doctors, chaplains, volunteer coordinators, volunteers, bereavement program coordinators, administrators—who shared with me their hard-won wisdom over the years. The dedicated professionals at Evergreen Hospice and Hospice of Seattle in Washington, Thedacare at Home/Hospice in Wisconsin, Hospice and Palliative Care Manitoba, Hospice Toronto, and Toronto Grace Health Centre Palliative Care help people live more fully through the end of life with humor, warmth, and passion that has been an inspiration.

I have been fortunate to find good people in Toronto who are passionately engaged with the written word. Thanks to the Canadian Authors Association, the Writers' Union of Canada, and the East-End Writers' Group for the many ways they offer encouragement to writers in all of our varied literary pursuits.

Nobody writes in a vacuum. I am grateful for the support of my friends and family who ask me for updates, listen to my rants, and share their own stories. You have held me steady through the craziness of writing, always ready to commiserate or celebrate as the occasion demanded. Thank you as well to my fellow dreamers at the International Association for the Study of Dreams, whose passion for dream work and research has opened me to new perspectives on dreaming.

Most of all I am grateful to my partner, Ann, whose love, support, and encouragement makes my writing possible in the first place. I am aware how rare a gift you have given me, and I promise not to waste a day of it.

Jeanne Van Bronkhorst

June 31, 2014

Introduction

Tallulah's father, Jerry, was dying a few years back. In his last week of life he was exhausted and frail. Caregivers watched over him night and day, helping him eat and rest and move a bit when he had energy. Nothing more could be done, and so the family settled in to keep watch. The end of life often looks like this, with no crisis, no pain, and no visible action. To everyone watching and maybe to himself—he looked like he had nothing left to do but wait to die. Then, in his final days, he had a dream that changed his life.

Jerry dreamed he was listening to his wife play the piano. Their marriage had been rocky and difficult, and they had separated several times over the years. His wife was a concert pianist before she died, nearly twenty years earlier. In Jerry's dream he sat in a large concert hall listening to exquisite piano music. Then he recognized the pianist was his wife, once again young and at the peak of her career, and his love and admiration for her came rushing back. He told Tallulah,

As music fills the room, I realize it is your mother who is playing, and I'm astounded at her beauty and the beauty

> *of the music. At the end of the first selection, I rise with*
> *everyone else and join in shouting, "Bravo! Bravo!"*

As Tallulah describes it, "Dad began to cry with joy as he told me the dream. His joy and shouting *bravo* triggered my own feeling of joy and gratitude that the dream seemed to bring everything into a sense of harmony."

This dream did not give Jerry advice for new treatments or change the course of his illness. He died a few days later. The dream changed his life nevertheless.

The dream took Jerry back to when his wife was strong, vibrant, and in her element. He recognized again her brilliance and her joy in creating beautiful music—a gift to her listeners. He saw her with kind eyes that no longer carried their fights and hurts. Instead, she shone with a pure and unadulterated brightness. He remembered and felt again his deep love for her that lay underneath all their troubles.

The dream helped Jerry feel at peace in his own life. He released some of the hurt and resentments he was still carrying and felt the relief of forgiveness for both his wife and himself.

Tallulah felt her own heart change as well as she listened to her father's dream. She saw in him a new capacity for love and peace, and it filled her with gratitude. "It felt like a great gift to me, and I could clearly see it was a gift for him."

Tallulah and her father were able to share that moment because they already knew how to talk to each other about their dreams. Tallulah worked with dreams for a living and has introduced group dream work into cancer treatment centers. She had talked with her father about dreams often enough that by the time he was dying he'd had some practice in remembering and telling his dreams.

Dreams like this one, which help us resolve long-standing hurts and appreciate old loves, can make us feel we are not approaching a final closure as much as we are stepping up to a sacred threshold. We linger a moment, suspended with our loved one between the demands of daily life and the unknown that awaits us, and our dreams linger with us. They help open our hearts right in the moments of our greatest fear, bringing a peaceful acceptance to the dying and relief and gratitude to the bereaved.

At the end of life, dreams can become powerful allies. Our dreams already know us intimately, having visited us every night of our lives. Throughout our days, dreams have given us insights and helped us solve problems, learn new tasks, create, play, and connect with friends. So it should be no surprise that when our lives are threatened by illness and our hearts are thrown into the chaos of dying, our dreams come forward to help again. When all else falls away, dreams come into a new urgency and a new beauty. At the end of life our dreams can bring us hope, comfort, and peace.

The Beginning of My Dream Appreciation

I gradually discovered the power of dreams over the ten years I was a hospice social worker. At first I ignored dreams, as do most social workers, doctors, nurses, and chaplains in health care. My home visits were filled with so many other important tasks that there wasn't time to ask clients and their families about dreams. I asked instead about their pain management, their eating and sleeping habits, and how they were all coping. I helped clients sign up for home-delivered meals, safety check-ins by phone, financial aid, and extra caregivers. I did notice we weren't talking about the bigger questions of whether life felt meaningful or what they believed in, but I hoped they were talking to each other about what really mattered when they were alone. Soon I discovered many clients and families could not bring themselves to talk about their deeper emotions, and I realized I needed another way to invite and open these important conversations.

One day I was visiting another client who had politely answered "fine, fine" to my questions about her emotional coping. Instead of moving on to the purpose for my visit, I decided to ask, "How are your dreams these days?"

She smiled and leaned back in her chair, then told me about a recent dream that gave her permission to quit her church volunteer position. She hadn't been able to quit before the dream because so many people relied on her. Her dream helped her to see she was getting tired and angry. She knew it was time to stop when she woke up from the dream. We talked then about church and her faith, responsibility and feeling useful, and how she was coping with the loss of this position.

That simple question launched me into a new relationship with clients and their dreams. Asking about dreams opened us easily into conversations about their most pressing concerns as well as the larger questions of life—conversations I had not found by asking about pain levels or eating habits. Some talked about their unique relationship with dreaming; some explained their philosophy of life. Sometimes a dream led clients to talk about how they understood their experience of illness and health. No matter the answer, the question moved us into a conversation about what mattered most to them in that moment, which made it easier to know what help they needed.

You may wonder, if dreams are such an amazing help at the end of life, why aren't more people working with dreams? Why has no one noticed this earlier? The answer has more to do with modern Western culture than with our dreams.

Most of us have been taught dreams aren't important or necessary for a good life, so we make no special effort to remember them. We keep too busy to spend much time thinking about something so unessential. Perhaps we've been frightened away by nightmares we would rather avoid. Of the people who are interested in dreams, most of us have been subtly warned to not enter into a dream's mysterious wilderness without a guide—a therapist, a dream worker, a facilitator—someone with a reliable map to the images we encounter.

The people who work in health care have heard these same warnings. Most are wary of asking about dreams when they have had no training in how to guide the discussion. One colleague of mine explained that since no one has yet developed an assessment tool or intervention protocol for dreams, she didn't feel comfortable asking about them. Even before these concerns, most health care professionals assume dreams are too compromised near the end of life by pain, illness, or medications to be of much help. They say those who are not already compromised don't have the energy for dreaming so why bother them with questions?

Even with all these understandable hesitations, something extraordinary happens when we pay attention to our dreams near the end of life. Whether we are the ones who are ill or the ones supporting someone we love, our dreams remind us we can find the inner strength to meet this last great mystery with courage and peace.

Over the years I developed a simple way to help people tell and appreciate their dreams. I made it safe for them to talk about dreams by inviting them to either talk about dreaming or to tell a dream. I asked simple questions: "What happened in the dream?" "How did you feel at the time?" "What does it remind you of?" I didn't offer an interpretation but instead let their dream and its meaning guide our conversation. I respected their ability to make sense of their experience and rarely heard a dream that was a complete mystery to the dreamer. The few times someone did offer a dream they could not make sense of, I shook my head along with them and we talked about how it feels to live alongside such baffling mysteries.

I quickly found this simple shared dream appreciation opened the very conversations that the people I met most needed to have. Their dreams opened a door to their most urgent concerns, their fondest hopes, and their deepest spiritual beliefs. Sometimes the dreams led us into the heart of what it means to be alive. During these conversations I have witnessed the remarkable support so many dreams offer at the end of life.

This book grew out my conversations with friends, colleagues, and clients across the United States and Canada. It is not meant to be an exhaustive study of every type of dream but rather an exploration of how dreams can help us at the end of life, if we give them room. For this reason, I've categorized the different dreams by how they help and not by their appearance. For instance, any dream that helps someone grieve can be a grief dream, regardless of the dream images. One dream might be of the person who died while another dream includes images that reflect a feeling of loss, separation, forgiveness, or guilt. The dreamer decides the purpose and the message of the dream.

The dreams I've included come from many different sources. I've drawn my examples from already-published works by other clinicians, researchers, and doctoral students, which are all referenced at the end of the book. I've interviewed friends and colleagues for their dreams, and I've included a few dreams from my own life. I have not used dreams of any individual clients from my hospice work, although I have included examples of dreams that draw upon my hospice experience. These dream examples are composites, describing dreams that share common images or meanings, and are not meant to describe any one individual.

Overview of the Book

I have divided the book into two parts. Part One explores how dreams can help the dying and the bereaved at the end of life. Whether dreams explore images of heaven or focus on the mundane tasks of daily life, they all can help dreamers cope with the end of life. For those who want to jump ahead, Part Two gives ideas on how best to listen to the dreams of loved ones and how to find your own dreams more easily.

At the end of each chapter I've added a summary and a few questions to help you think and talk about your own experience with dreams. I've included the questions I've asked myself and my own friends and family, and I hope they can help you start conversations with people you trust.

In chapters 1 and 2, I talk about how dreams draw upon and help illuminate the daily cares and challenges everyone faces at the end of life. Dreams can also remind us of what we want most from each other. Many people find it too difficult to say the words "I am dying" or "I am frightened of losing you." Dreams can help by putting these strong emotions into images and storylines that are less direct. It is much easier to share a story than a raw emotion.

Chapters 3 and 4 explore dreams of people who are dying. People near the end of life often dream of business that needs to be finished and relationships that need resolution. Other dreams prepare the dreamer for a journey, and they wake with images of packing, finding their tickets, or boarding a ship. Visitation dreams also become more common at the very end of life. People who are dying are visited by loved ones who have already died and now bring messages of comfort and hope. After the death, families cherish these visitation dreams.

Chapters 5 and 6 consider the dreams of family and friends. Very few people will ever die truly alone, even if no one is physically present at their bedside. Most people are connected to a web of family (both close and distant), friends, colleagues, a spiritual community, book clubs, hunting buddies, teammates, and neighbors, any whom might be affected enough to dream about the person or their own grief. These dreams help families and friends prepare for loss or help them say goodbye. Sometimes people dream of their friend visiting them and wake to find the person died that same night. The idea of loved ones visiting our dreams after they have died has grown so popular that many people seek out counseling if they don't dream of their loved one. I have also included a chapter about dreams that frighten us and how you can learn to respond to them with courage and good humor (see chapter 7).

Part One ends with a chapter on other common-but-mysterious happenings at the moment of death, such as synchronicities and animals acting out of character. These moments aren't dreams, but they often feel dreamlike. In the midst of our waking day, the physical world suddenly reveals itself to be deeply connected with our emotional and spiritual life, and as a result many people feel less alone in the universe (see chapter 8).

Part Two begins with chapter 9, which explores how best to listen to the dreams of people you love. Chapter 10 will help you to learn to remember your own dreams more consistently and will show you how to develop a trusting relationship with them. These two chapters will help you give your dreams all the invitation they need to come back into your waking life.

Dreams at the end of life, no matter what images they bring, seem to bring a deep reassurance of our life's meaning, purpose, and ultimate worth. The epilogue explores how this reassurance affects dreamers and family alike and why it is so important to all of our lives.

Three Levels of Dream Appreciation

Throughout this book, I've paid attention to three different levels at which we can interact with dreams at the end of life. First, the dream images themselves are often clear and direct, perhaps more direct than at other times in life. They don't need in-depth interpretation as much as they need to be experienced and treasured. Every chapter is filled with dream images and how they can speak directly to the dreamer's life. Tallulah's father, Jerry, didn't have to interpret his dream to feel a rush of appreciation and love for his wife. He woke up with those feelings still strong in him.

The second level of dream appreciation considers a dream's power when we tell it out loud. When Jerry told Tallulah about his dream, he had the chance to re-experience it, crying in joy again, and feeling its powerful emotions resolve his feelings for his wife. The simple act of telling a dream also helps dreamers understand it better because they are turning images into a story with a plot and meaning. Telling a dream invites us to make sense of it and add our interpretation, which in turn helps build our confidence with future dreams. Telling a dream strengthens the emotional bonds between dreamer and listener no matter what the dream is about. A dream that is told out loud can become a gift to an entire community. Jerry's dream and his response to the dream helped Tallulah feel relief and peace when she saw her father so caught up in this final exchange.

When telling a dream, the dreamer momentarily slips the bonds of being the patient, the caregiver, or the child and instead becomes the storyteller. The dreamer offers something odd, quaint, powerful, delightful, or puzzling as a gift in the form of a story to the rest of the family. One dream can help everyone involved connect with each other again on the deepest human level. I have seen a single dream pull strangers together into a community and a family into a team.

On the third and deepest level of dream appreciation, dreams help remind people of their dignity and worth at the time when their dignity and worth are most often in doubt. Dreams do this by drawing the dreamer's attention back to their life's fundamental purpose and meaning. All too often at the end of life the attention of everyone remains fixed on the physical care needs of the person who is ill. Taking good care of someone is important, but when their bodies become dependent on the ministrations of others, many people struggle to find the purpose in their life and some become despondent. The power of a dream's insistence on personal growth and insight can help sustain a person's reason for living until the very end. Tallulah's father's dream all but ignored the fact he had no more physical energy and was waiting to die. Instead the dream focused on what he still had to learn and how he could still grow as an individual.

As we draw closer to death, our dreams become more insistent that we are alive and will go on living, learning, and loving as long as we breathe and, perhaps, long after that. Our dreams remain our own—creative, bold, willful, and fully charged by an inner fire.

Jerry used his last days on earth to mend his relationship with his wife. Even though she had been gone for more than twenty years, even though he had only days to live, his dream brought him a new (old) emotional challenge. In doing so, his dream let him know that what he felt and thought about his life still mattered. In his dream he wasn't waiting to die. Within his dream he was busy and engaged and still working at growth. He was reviewing his life, reconnecting with his loved one, changing his heart, and giving all this transformation and new possibility to his daughter as a parting gift.

How Real Are Dreams?

Most dream experts agree that everyone dreams. Dreams have been noted in all cultures in all times through the course of human history. Anthropologists believe the earliest cave paintings may very well have depicted important dreams. Dreams are common to all mammals, not just humans, as anyone with a pet can attest. What our dogs and cats dream about we will never know, but we can see their muscles twitch and hope they are happily chasing squirrels, who may in turn be dreaming of discovering hidden nut caches.

Outside of Western culture, dreams are considered both important and essential to daily life. Dr. Charles Laughlin, emeritus professor of anthropology and religion at Carleton University, notes the existence of more than four thousand cultures in the world today, and more than 90 percent of those cultures place a high value on dreams.[1]

Inside Western culture, however, the role of dreams underwent a fundamental shift. After thousands of years in which everyone in Western culture knew dreams to be direct conduits to a divine realm, Christians began linking dreams to demonic possession as a way to differentiate themselves from followers of the old Pagan beliefs. Soon after that, the Age of Enlightenment ushered in a new, scientific way of exploring the world. As a result, the importance of dreams and dreaming became less certain.

---

1. Charles D. Laughlin, *Communing with the Gods: Consciousness, Culture and the Dreaming Brain* (Australia: Daily Grail, 2011), 64.

Stanley Krippner, Fariba Bogzaran, and André Percia de Carvalho follow the progression of Western culture's understanding of dreams in their book, *Extraordinary Dreams and How to Work with Them*. Krippner and his colleagues chart a narrowing of focus as Western culture moved into the Age of Enlightenment. "Over the millennia, the source of dreams has been seen as divine, demonic, the dreamer's 'soul,' the dreamer's environment, the dreamer's unconscious, the dreamer's imagination, and the dreamer's brain." [2]

What was once revered as a spiritual connection to a divine reality has gradually been reduced in our imaginations into a fairly random event happening strictly within our brain. Today, much of dream research centers on the neurological process of dreaming.

Despite this narrow focus, many people find their dreams gain a new immediacy and meaning at the end of life. Researchers often report their study participants tell them these end-of-life dreams feel vivid and real in a way their usual dreams do not. Some dreams feel more objectively real than their own imagination, and that realness spurs some people into a deeper faith or spiritual belief. The moments feel transcendent, as if they connect the dreamer directly to a loving afterlife.

These dreams and moments seem to answer the question people have been asking ever since people knew how to ask it: *What happens when we die?* The world's religions, great and small, all offer a vision of what comes next. The vision may

---

2. Stanley Krippner, Fariba Bogzaran, and André Percia de Carvalho, *Extraordinary Dreams and How to Work with Them* (New York: SUNY Press, 2002), 20.

be of heavenly realms of angels singing; ashes returning to feed the earth's next generation; tearful, joyful reunions; or reincarnation with ultimate enlightenment. Existential philosophers teach that every person ultimately faces this question alone. Scientists stop at the edge of physical death and solemnly pronounce that science can look no further. At the end of life, doctors and nurses describe how the organs shut down and what kind of sensations the dying person might feel because of the physical process, but they won't allow their speculation to go past the physical body.

Our dreams are not so careful. They rush right into and through the end of life, and they show us life continuing after death in a way that shakes dreamers and all who hear their stories with a marvelous, wondrous certainty. People who are dying see long-deceased relatives visiting them in dreams or when awake, and these visitors appear real. Not a dream, a memory, or a hallucination, but truly there in the room. Family members dream of saying goodbye to a loved one and wake to find that person died suddenly that very same night, and they feel sure that person visited them. People in grief find the world flooded with small events that connect to their personal loss in a way that feels deeply meaningful.

This book explores the question of what dreams can do for us at the most difficult, frightening, overwhelming time in our lives. As you move through the book, keep in mind that it is not intended to tell you what you or your loved one should be experiencing, or what you should believe. Every person is different, and many dream experts have noticed that each person's dreams will remain faithful to the dreamer's own perspective on life and death. My fondest hope is that it gives you a new appreciation for your dreams and helps you trust your dreams enough to listen to them when you need them most. I believe dreams can help dreamers and their entire families face the end of life with more hope, comfort, and courage.

When we can no longer walk, when we have trouble talking, and when our breathing begins to falter, we can still dream. We can hold our dear ones in our dreams, wish them well, say goodbye over and over, and touch them one last time. We close our physical eyes and our dreams reach out across the unknown future to give us glimpses of light and loving company and something beautiful that lies beyond.

Part One: How Dreams Help at the End of Life

Throughout our lives dreams reflect what is closest to our hearts. They touch on the mundane tasks we fuss over, provide insights, revisit important relationships and past events, and help us sort through complex problems. Most dreams at the end of life are like dreams at any other time. Some people will remember only confusing fragments while others wake from dreams that carry powerful, healing messages.

What makes dreams at the end of life different—richer, more meaningful, more helpful—is precisely the fact that the end of life is one of the most intense, stressful, meaningful, and sacred times we will ever face. Dreams at the end of life are more helpful than dreams at other times because we are more in need of their help. The threat of immeasurable loss can make our time together all the more precious. The threat of nonexistence makes our dreams reach out to explore and then describe to us how we may very well continue on, and how we can survive the loss we must now face.

Not all dreams help in the same way, and some dreams will never make much sense to the dreamer, but it is clear that all dreams carry the potential to help. We can take comfort from their images and we can lean on them to talk with the people we love most.

Chapter One

Dreams Support
Our Waking Lives

Dreams don't need to show us visions of the afterlife to help us live with greater peace at the end of life. Many dreams do nothing more than amplify our concerns in waking life. People who are ill also dream about pain, living with new limitations, or making a list of what they still want to do. Caregivers might dream of being overwhelmed by natural disasters, taking long vacations, or struggling to meet the needs of family members. The dream images help people remember again what they most need from life at this time, and they sometimes offer ways to meet those needs.

Focus on What Is Important Right Now

Fiona Martins, a palliative care nurse in Toronto, helps people manage their final illnesses in their homes.[3] She loves her work and often feels honored to be allowed into such a tender moment. She has seen how dreams help her clients and their

---

3. Fiona Martins, palliative care nurse with Community Care Access Center. All quotes from Fiona are from my telephone interview with her in Toronto, Ontario, in November 2012.

families focus on what is most important to them. Like all good nurses in palliative care, Martins focuses her attention on pain and symptom management. Her job is to make sure people are comfortable enough to remain independent in their homes for as long as possible.

At each visit she asks them to give a number between one and ten to describe the level of their pain. She asks about any new symptoms, any side effects from the medications, and how they are eating and sleeping. Her sleep assessment focuses on the physical aspects of sleep. Martins asks: Are they in too much pain to sleep? Do they have anxiety that keeps them up at night? Have their medicines interfered with their sleep cycle? Are they hallucinating? If the answer to any of these questions is yes, she can often alleviate the problem with a simple change in medicine.

Martins doesn't routinely ask about dreams, but she finds people will occasionally offer their dreams to her without her asking. When her clients tell her about a dream, she listens closely. Martins has never been trained in dream analysis, but she has learned dreams often speak directly to the daily troubles her clients might be having but are unable to describe. She trusts that anyone who is telling her a dream is telling her for a reason, and she looks at each dream through the lens of her work. A man tells her he dreamed the medicine was really poison and woke up in a sweat the next morning. Rather than brushing the dream away as nothing more than anxiety, Martins decides they should both go through all his medication again, carefully checking the strength and the timing of each dose. She takes his dream seriously as being one way he can express his concern. A different client's caregiver insists to Martins she is fine, but Martins can see she is exhausted. Then the caregiver tells Martins she has dreamed of being lost and alone on a sinking life raft, and Martins helps her reconsider whether she has enough help at home. She helps the woman think of her dream as a gift, bringing her a vivid picture of emotions she hadn't known she was feeling.

The dreams Martins describes here are not pleasant ones, but they serve an important purpose. They remind us our dreams are often like watchdogs, faithful guardians that help us recognize and say aloud what we need most, right now, even if we haven't been able to identify those needs before. The dreams throw a spotlight on our own unconscious assessment of how we are doing physically and emotionally. When Martins responds to these dreams as meaningful and important, she gives her clients permission to trust that their dreams are working for them, even though the dreams themselves might be upsetting.

Bring Respite from Suffering

Dreaming is one of the few activities we can do well even when every other activity falls away. In dreams people long confined to wheelchairs can run along sandy beaches, reveling in the feel of the wind against their face and the sun on their back. I have seen people who have not moved easily in months wake from such dreams and move their bodies with more confidence and a new boldness, as if the dreams refreshed their sense of physical power.

Dreams can take people away from their current suffering, at least momentarily. They may only be dreams, destined to fade against the harsher reality of suffering, but sometimes the emotional effects of respite dreams linger into the day. Some dreams change waking life for the better. Daniel, my friend's father, had respite dreams just like these.

Before his illness, Daniel was a quiet man in his mid-sixties who spent much of his working life alone, repairing phone lines across his province. When he was diagnosed with a rare form of brain cancer, he and his family were devastated. The cancer gave him an unrelenting parade of small strokes that incapacitated him. He needed constant supervision and, after a lifetime of working independently, Daniel found himself living in a locked hospital unit, unable to go home, often unable to clearly remember his home, and waiting for nursing home placement. The speed in which his life narrowed from home, work, and family to this one long-term care unit was heartbreaking. The strokes pushed him into a lurching dementia with moments of terrible confusion alternating with more lucid moments that were filled with grief and despair.

The hospital staff tried to help him with medications and friendly support, but he often sat without moving or speaking to them, hopeless and depressed. Daniel's wife, Angela, visited him every day, but it was tough on her as well. He didn't remember enough for a conversation with her, and sometimes he didn't remember her at all. She grieved over their lost life together and felt guilty leaving him each evening. Friends came to visit Daniel, but they, too, found it hard to watch him suffer. He couldn't remember his life with them outside the hospital, and it didn't take long before their visits tapered off. Everyone was miserable.

Then one morning Daniel greeted his wife with a wide smile. "Last night," he said, "I went dancing." He looked pleased with himself and immensely satisfied, and he wanted to tell her all about it.

At first Angela argued with him. She knew he hadn't been out dancing. She knew it was the brain tumor causing him to confuse reality with fantasy. She wanted him to remember where he was now and remember her and their life together, but all he wanted to do that day was talk about things she knew could not have happened. The next day he described a different adventure, also involving friends and dancing. A few days later he described going out to dinner to a nice restaurant.

In times past, many hospital staff would have looked for ways to curtail dreams like Daniel's. They might have encouraged Angela to reorient Daniel back to his present, no matter how painful, and help him through his depression with more and better medication. But this hospital staff noticed Daniel looked brighter, more calm and relaxed, and pleased with his new memories. Wherever he had been the night before in his dreams, he returned convinced he'd had a great time.

After long discussions, Angela and the hospital staff decided to listen to Daniel instead of medicating him or talking him out of his experiences. They began wishing him good dreams at night, and then asking for a report the next morning. The staff always asked him what he had dreamed, but Daniel's family and friends went a step further. They asked him what he had been *doing*. They let go of the need to orient him back to the reality of his situation and instead let him expound on his nightly adventures. For the next six months, life opened up for all of them.

Daniel's dream adventures never veered into outright fantasy. He didn't fight dragons or become a super spy or fly to other planets. Instead he enjoyed a more social life than he had ever had before being admitted to the hospital. Before his illness, he came home for dinner every evening, watched a little television with his wife, maybe talked to his children by phone, and was in bed by ten p.m. But now he regaled staff and visitors with his tales of dancing, dinners, staying out late, and having deep conversations with old friends.

My friend Craig, Daniel's adult son, describes the change with affection and relief:

> *He went out one night with friends to the beach and then out to dinner. He went to the circus one time, they had a good time and went to dinner after. Always out to dinner after. I ask him, "And what time did you get home?" and he tells me, "About three or four in the morning. Oh yes, I am very busy." He went skydiving once and he has all these details: the location of the airport, how much gas it cost to get out there, the hour it took to fly up high enough. So it's always something really nice.*

Daniel's dreams gave him fun experiences he could hang on to during his day. In his dreams he took physical and emotional risks he never took before his illness. He reconnected with friends he hadn't seen in decades. He enjoyed himself, living with an energy and taste for the nightlife his family didn't recognize.

I was drawn to Daniel's story in part because there was no question his dreams were coming from his imagination alone. Nobody except Daniel believed he was actually out dancing with his old friends, most of whom were alive and visiting him during the day. His dreams helped him despite being induced by his illness. And because they helped him, rather than distressing or confusing him, the medical team allowed him to continue dreaming. The doctors and nurses and family came to view these dreams as part of what helped Daniel, even though the dreams could be considered a symptom of disease. Daniel's story shows that where our dreams originate matters less than what our dreams can do for us.

This point will become even more important later in the book. People too often feel pushed to verify their dreams as objectively real before they can accept the comfort of a dream's message. Daniel's story reminds us that if a dream brings respite or comfort or a challenge the dreamer can meet, then the dream is helpful, no matter where it comes from.

Research has shown that what we imagine has the effect of lighting up the same regions in our brains as our memories of actual events. The impact of an imaginary adventure might not have the same lasting impact as a memory of a *real* event, but both imagined and real memory trace along the same neural pathways and release the same chemicals. Athletes and performers use this similarity to help them imagine their routines before they begin a competition, seeing it in their minds and letting their muscles respond to the pleasure of working well.

Daniel didn't need to remember he had merely been dreaming. In fact, Daniel confusing his dreams for waking experiences might actually have done him some good. Because he didn't see his nightly adventures as dreams, he had no need to dismiss them as unreal. He could accept them as genuine experiences, and he got the same benefit (although less intense) from them as if he really had been out dancing or skydiving or dining with friends.

It wasn't long before Daniel's dreams changed his daily routine for the better. He no longer fretted about not being home because he could remember being out the night before and had something to look forward to the next evening. Angela slowly learned to relax into her husband's new life. She missed her husband remembering her, but she could see he was no longer suffering. Even if he didn't remember their life together, she found she enjoyed listening to his stories. She loved seeing him pain free and clearly reveling in his life. She remarked with bemusement more than once, "He's having a better life than I am. I just go home and go to bed each night while he's out gallivanting."

Bring Families Together

One of the great challenges of living through our dying is to open ourselves to each other and connect with each other on an emotional and spiritual level. Some people build that emotional connection with family through their faith; they pray together, read the holy books, and talk about their hopes for the life to come. Others find the physical act of caregiving—the intimate acts of washing someone's body, supporting them as they walk, lifting them, and helping them eat—brings them into an emotional intimacy they had never before imagined. The physical closeness leads to emotional bonding as two people journey on a single path.

Sharing dreams—even when we don't agree on what the dreams are or where they come from—can be another way to build this emotional closeness. Any dream, big or small, meaningful or nonsensical, can help build precious connections with families when the dreams are shared.

Daniel's dreams gave him a chance to practice talking with others, and he grew to truly enjoy the company of other people. Before Daniel got sick, he and his wife rarely went out with friends or other family. When he first became ill and his family rallied around him, he was often uncomfortable. He didn't have much practice in small talk, and all the visiting exhausted him.

Daniel's dreams changed that dynamic. In his dreams he reached out socially, hung out with old friends, had long conversations over dinner, and was rewarded with friendships he enjoyed. The dreams helped him build skills that he then brought back with him into his waking life. He found it much easier to talk and laugh with the people who came to visit him, even if he wasn't always sure who they were. It didn't take long for his extended family and old friends to learn they could engage with this newly sociable person. His friends returned as their conversations could now center on his adventures. They were able to make a new connection with him based on his dream memories.

Daniel's dreams gave him another few months of emotional connection with the people he loved. To his family and the staff, Daniel's dreams became a welcome relief from the strain of his illness. His dreams gave them all new memories that they will cherish and laugh over in their grief for the rest of their lives.

Daniel's story introduces another important benefit of dreams at the end of life. Before his dreams began, Daniel was no longer contributing to his family. He couldn't provide for his wife, and he couldn't live at home safely. He couldn't remember his family and friends enough to reminisce or engage in any meaningful conversation. He needed help for every aspect of his life.

But when he started telling his dreams, part of that suffering lifted. Through his dream sharing he began contributing to the conversation again. He had a story to tell; he had something to offer. His dreams carried new stories and through them he became an active member of his family once more. Researchers consider this an instance of social reciprocity and a good measure of human dignity. Each person involved had something important to contribute. Daniel again had something to say that others were glad to hear.

Reflect on Life's Meaning

One of the great psychological tasks at the end of life is to reflect on what our lives have meant. People talk with family and caregivers about what their life has meant, what it means now, what they want to be remembered for, and what it was all about. They think: I was a good parent. I was always responsible. My children know I've loved them. I always knew how to find adventure. I am a child of God. I know I've had a good life. I've been a survivor. I did my best. I messed up, but I can see it all turned out for the best. I tried to do what is right. I was the black sheep of the family, the truth teller, the one who got out, the good daughter. I loved being a teacher (farmer, mother, engineer, dancer). I always wished I had become a scientist (doctor, father, athlete, painter).

There are so many ways we express this last summing up of our lives and so many ways to enter those precious conversations. Sometimes I've asked people outright, "What has life been all about for you?" Sometimes I've asked people to tell me about important moments in their life and how these moments shaped the rest of their life. Hospice workers and volunteers call it a life review, but families simply call it sharing stories or passing on lessons to the next generation.

Our dreams can help us ease into this reflective frame of mind. *I dream of my childhood and spend the day thinking about those early days. I dream of old friends and remember them during the day, thinking about what the friendships mean to me.* I met a woman once who told me she had dreamed about painting again, something she had done in high school but had given up after graduation. The dream reminded her of her younger self's fantasies of being a famous artist. It was so vivid, she told me, she could almost smell the oils on the canvas. I asked her what the dream reminded her of, and she talked about her decision to give up painting. She told me life got hard, paint was expensive, and she no longer had the time. She paused a minute, considering. "Actually," she continued, "I stopped because I needed to get married, and then when I had my kids nothing else mattered. I'd do anything for those kids. My youngest just got married, did I tell you that? And I'm a grandma three times over."

Her dream helped her revisit one of the major turning points in her life, when she turned from being a painter to becoming a wife and mother. The dream gave her time to think again about that decision, now with the benefit of hindsight, and she realized she would make the same decision over again.

She was doing soul work—reflecting on major life decisions and how they had shaped her life. I have seen many dreams like this one help people reflect on decisions they have made. The dreams show our decisions good and bad, our plans followed or compromised, and how it all turned out.

Comfort a Community

Some dreams can help entire communities provide comfort and hope to each other. When a dream is shared, its story reaches out to the listeners as well as the dreamers. The dreams help families build a new language of hope for themselves and their loved ones. Social work professor Dr. Michele Chaban gives an example of this healing power.[4]

During her long career in hospice and palliative care, Chaban helped develop a palliative care program at Mount Sinai Hospital in Toronto called the Temmy Latner Center. Chaban knows a child's dream of a peaceful and happy afterlife could help everyone surrounding that small person. She taught children and their families to look for their dreams, and she helped the children talk about the dreams they remembered. She did this using the same open-ended dream appreciation I have used with adults. As much as she explained the importance of dreams to the families of the sick children, she didn't offer any specific interpretations. She says,

---

4. Dr. Michele Chaban, codirector of the Applied Mindfulness Meditation Certificate at Factor-Inwentash Faculty of Social Work. All quotes from Michele are from our telephone interview in November 2012.

We are learning from their experience rather than interpreting the dream. We are just asking them to reflect on what it felt like to them. I would ask them questions like, "What do you think that was about?" These were mostly kids who didn't have a lot of social or emotional experience of what dying was or what being sick was. But they could describe their dream. They could say, "I had a dream last night, I was in this beautiful space ..."

The following example is drawn from her many years of experience.

> *A seven-year-old girl near the end of her life wakes one afternoon from a dream in which she visited a beautiful place. In the dream, her grandmother, many years dead, enveloped her in a welcoming hug. She excitedly tells her parents that she can still feel her grandmother's arms and smell her perfume.*

Chaban has known many people who have had such a beautiful dream. Beyond the welcome sensation of being held and loved, the dream carries an emotional depth. The little girl tells her parents, "I feel safe. She's waiting for me."

I will explore dreams like this in later chapters, but for now I want to focus on how such a dream affects the life of dreamers and their families. The girl wakes up feeling more confident in her future, more hopeful, and maybe safe enough to be a little curious about what is to come. Her dream of her grandmother helps her move toward a future she can now envision, one that holds and comforts her.

Chaban knows even such a comforting dream will help only as long as it is remembered. So Chaban helps all her young patients tell the dream to their parents and anyone they trust. By sharing the dream they remember it over and over, and each time they can feel again its comfort.

These dreams then bring comfort to the parents and anyone who hears them. Watching a child die has to be one of the worst events of any parent's life. How helpless do parents feel when they watch their child live with pain and fear and know they can do nothing to relieve it? When their child draws peace and courage from a dream such as this one, the parents are given strength and peace as well.

For those who believe in an afterlife, the arrival of their own deceased mother in a dream brings enormous relief and comfort. Suddenly they are not alone but part of a loving transfer team, and the moment of death—as painful as it inevitably must be—holds more hope and peace than they had thought possible.

Those parents who don't believe in an afterlife can still see their child is no longer suffering in the same way and no longer feels afraid, alone, or abandoned. They can see her reaching out toward something more, something next, and can hope her final moments will include more calm and peace. And that is worth everything.

The dream gives everyone involved a chance to offer comfort by participating in the dream. Chaban explains, "The family and the medical team can say to the child who is dying,

'You've had the dream, go to that special place in your dream.' So then everybody starts to use it in a way that is creating peace and hope—a little bit of optimism." The entire community that surrounds this child has a way to help her feel held even as she leaves them. The dream gives the medical team a precious tool they can use to bring comfort, which brings them relief and comfort as well.

Chapter Summary

Our dreams help us live more fully, even at—especially at—the end of life. Perhaps for the first time dreamers find within ourselves a trusted ally. Our dreams remind us of what we know is most important. Dreams can bring us temporary respite from our pain and fear and remind us of our strength. Dreams help us reflect on life's meaning when we revisit past decisions and important relationships. One dream image can comfort an entire community when all else seems lost and help soften grief over the years. We dream of something better waiting for us just beyond our sight and wake up feeling hopeful, curious, and ready to move forward. Dreams can do all this and more when we allow them room in our life and by talking about them with people we trust.

Talking about dreams does more than simply help us remember their details. Dreams can also help us with the important, difficult conversations so many people long to have at the end of life but don't know how to begin. Telling our dreams can bring us closer to the people we love and give us a lasting message of hope.

Talking about Dreams

- What role have your dreams played in your life so far?

- What do you think has influenced your relationship with your dreams?

- Daniel's family encouraged him to believe his dreams were actually his waking life. What circumstances might lead you to make the same choice with someone you love?

- Has a dream ever helped you resolve a problem or a question in your daily life? How did the dream help?

Chapter Two

Dreams Open
Important Conversations

Monique Seguin is a licensed practical nurse who works in an inpatient hospice unit in a small Quebec town. Seguin often works with people who are in their final few days of life. She sees them when they can no longer remain safely at home, even with help, and she is busy keeping them safe and out of pain. Like me, Seguin has noticed that her conversations with patients, like most conversations between people and their caregivers at the end of life, too often are limited to questions about their various bodily functions. She says:

> The questions [nurses] ask all the time are did you eat well, sleep well, how is your bowel working, what is your pain level [on a scale] from 1–10? Those are the only four questions we ask. After so many [times being asked, the patients] get fed up with it.[5]

---

5. Monique Seguin, licensed practical nurse in palliative care. All quotes from Monique are from my telephone interview with her in November 2012.

Seguin had been interested in her own dreams for years and now wondered if her patients were still dreaming in their final days. So she began asking patients if they dreamed.

What she discovered startled her. She found the people she was caring for physically also had emotional lives that could be shared and cherished in the short time they had left. "If you walk in and ask, 'Do you dream? Have you had a dream?' It makes a big difference! It's another subject to talk about," she said.

What she offers is a simple invitation to share their dreams, much like my invitation. As she helps her patients get ready for bed, she asks them if they dream. She doesn't offer interpretations, but she listens calmly and lets the dreams speak for themselves. She has collected more than a hundred dreams in this way and, with her patients' permission, she published a small book about dreams and the end of life.[6] Seguin says, "I think what they're getting from the dream is where they are in their soul, their heart, their emotions. For my work it is the best tool that I have. Even if the dream doesn't look important, it opens a door to communication."

The benefit of dream appreciation lies in its simplicity. It needs only a small step of bringing our dreams back into conversation where they can do us all some good. Dreams that are shared help bring more dream details to mind and give the dreamer room to ponder the dreams' connections to waking life. The dreams might help the us prepare for death, or they might simply remind us of easier times.

---

6. Nicole Gratton and Monique Seguin, *Dreams and Death: The Benefits of Dreams Before, During, and After Death* (Canada: Gratton and Seguin, 2011).

This chapter is all about dreams that help open conversations at the end of life. I have met many people over the years who have sat by their loved ones' side and not known what to say. Some have wanted to talk about important end-of-life matters but couldn't find a way to bring up such delicate topics. Others have searched for anything to talk about and come away feeling frustrated, too fearful of saying the wrong thing to say anything at all. What to talk about and when to begin these conversations are difficult questions to answer.

I also want to acknowledge, before going any further, that some people who are ill do not want to talk about what is happening to them. They are certain they will have a better life if they can ignore their illness as long as possible and focus instead on what they can still enjoy. There is a lot of life remaining between a fatal diagnosis and the final hours, and some people want all that life focused on living. They consciously give up putting their lives in order so they can live their fullest life as long as possible. Some may fear that talking about what is happening will make their remaining time that much worse.

Families often worry this avoidance is all part of an unhealthy denial, but for many people this avoidance works to give them their best version of life, which is as healthy as anything gets. As a hospice worker I have seen people avoid talking about their illness long enough to have one last grand adventure, and they have died satisfied and at peace with their decision.

People who want to avoid talking about their illness may feel they have to avoid their dreams as well, but that isn't necessary. Dreams won't force dreamers to consider what someone else thinks is best for them against their own wishes. Dreams help us all have our best lives in whatever way we define our best lives to be. Dreams can offer the thrilling adventures that Daniel enjoyed in chapter 1, or recall quieter, more meaningful past moments.

Asking about dreams is one way to move beyond the pains of the immediate moment into a new conversation, whether the conversation is about just the dream or how the dream connects to life in general. Dreams can give dreamers and listeners a moment of escapist joy as they recount their more nonsensical adventures, and dreams can help people gingerly wade into the delicate but frightening, unsettling emotions that swirl around the end of life.

Help Us Talk about Life

Asking people about their dreams can open up a new world of possible conversations. My question to clients and family members—*How are your dreams these days?*—often gives people a chance to talk about what they think and feel about the life they are leading. Just as there is no single, perfect dream that everyone should have, so there is no single, right way to relate to our dreams. My question sometimes opened a philosophical conversation on their views about dreaming, where again I found a wide range of responses.

- I'm an atheist; I don't think about dreams.
- God answers my prayers in my dreams.
- My dreams have been more vivid lately.
- I never remember my dreams.

Each response led to a new conversation about what dreaming and life in general means to them. My question could be considered an invitation to a casual conversation. It is the kind of question we might ask about work or family, as in "How are your parents?" Our conversations about dreaming are deeper than casual chats about the weather, but they are less threatening than direct questions about emotions.

Most people have an opinion about what dreams mean, regardless of whether they remember their dreams. Those who don't think about dreams still feel invited into a conversation that has nothing to do with their illness or symptoms, which can be its own relief. For those who do remember their dreams, talking about them gives the dream new vitality and importance. Sharing a dream makes it more real and helps connect it more firmly with the dreamer's life.

Dreams don't always have to lead to the big conversations of life; sometimes they give dreamers permission to voice concerns they might be afraid to bring up. Even difficult dreams, such as *I dreamed I had to move to a nursing home that was ugly and smelled awful and I woke up crying,* are invitations to talk about how life is now for the dreamer. This dreamer might be expressing for the first time her fear of being forced out of her home. Maybe she wants to talk about the help she needs and the independence she can't lose, or maybe she is beginning the hard work of preparing herself for moving. When someone shares such a poignant dream, I take extra time to explore what it means for the dreamer. The dream offers another way the dreamer can tell me about what matters most to her.

Sometimes people dream about their childhood:

- *I was sitting by the river that ran behind my house when I was a kid, and all my friends were sitting on the other side.*

- *I dreamed about the farm I grew up on—I forgot how beautiful it was.*

- *I was five again, running along the beach with my big sister.*

The dreamer might be ready to reminisce about those places and people or ponder how they and the world had changed since then. Whatever dreams they choose to tell me, I keep in mind their dreams are a starting point for whatever they want to discuss. *I dreamed my oldest daughter came back and was looking for my help* might lead to the admission, "I wish I could see her again." Or the dreamer could be getting ready to tell me more about her eldest daughter or about what has separated them for so long or how close they have always been.

Each dream is an invitation to talk about what these days are like for them, what they want, and who they love. They help people review their lives, the important moments, the happy or traumatic memories, and the choices they made. The dreams don't need to provide answers as much as help launch dreamers into a new conversation about what is weighing on their minds.

The dreams I heard were rarely told for my benefit alone. Most often families and caregivers were also present, and the dreams became a way to help them talk to each other about their lives. Too often families had no idea so much was going on inside their loved ones' minds. The daily demands of caring for the physical needs of another human being can easily take up all a person's time and energy, leaving little room for the emotional sharing so many people treasure. The illness often pushes everyone—client and family alike—into a tight circle of attention on the physical body. Families and caregivers have wondered aloud to me, "What did we talk about before we had to talk about symptoms and medicine?" If left unremarked, the gap between what people want to say and what they allow themselves to say can widen into a chasm. Dreams open conversations that help narrow that gap again.

As listeners, our main task is to listen to what the dream means to the dreamer. By letting the dreamer interpret the dream, we can find our way into the conversation they need to have with us. A war veteran might tell me, *I dreamed about the war, and I was running under fire again.* This dream doesn't have one precise meaning that I can teach him. It is his dream and his decision to tell me this particular dream, so what I can do best is trust he offers this dream to begin a conversation with me. I have to wait for what that conversation will be. Perhaps he wants to talk about his experience in the military or his philosophy of fighting or how it felt being under fire back then and how the dream reminds him he is feeling under fire now. Perhaps the dream reminds him of decisions he has made in his life that he now regrets or feels most proud of. Perhaps his dream helps him understand better his feelings now about his family. As long as I don't jump in with an interpretation, his dream becomes his own unique path into a conversation with me.

Help Us Talk about Strong Emotions

Ira Byock, MD, is a well-known hospice medical director and best-selling author of *Dying Well: Peace and Possibilities at the End of Life.* In the book, he lists what he considers the four most important things we can tell each other at the end of life: I love you, I forgive you, please forgive me, and thank you. These are powerful messages, and they are all messages from the heart. Love and forgiveness, gratitude and letting go are the work of the soul rather than the body. While Byock acknowledges not everyone can say these things aloud, he still wants to help people find the words. He knows what mental health clinicians and counselors and hospice professionals have begun to prove in research—we connect and reconcile with each other through conversations. True intimacy grows when we allow our inner lives to be seen, when we can trust we are safe in the good wishes of our listener, and when we can hold them in turn with our care and respect. At the end of life, these emotional ties become even more important.

Unfortunately, it's not easy to find our way into these emotional conversations. As important as it is to share emotions at the end of life, very few people can bring them up easily with the people they love. Dying can frighten us, and the complex and contradictory emotions we experience can feel a little too out of control for us to handle in a conversation.

The idea that talking about strong emotions can help both speaker and listener lead better lives is not new. In the past forty years, support groups were developed in large part because people who faced extraordinary circumstances needed someplace to talk about their experience away from their families. Support groups offer a safe place where people can share their perspectives and emotions that might otherwise make friends or families uncomfortable. In my city right now there are support groups for people with cancer, families of people with dementia, survivors of suicide, people in grief, and people living with a range of chronic or life-threatening illnesses.

The strength of support groups lies in the willingness of members to be vulnerable with each other, which is also their greatest challenge. Most of these support groups were designed specifically to give people room to talk about the emotions they can't share with their families or friends, and still a surprising number of support group members across the country won't bring up such frightening subjects as dying, grief, loss, or the fears they live with every day.

Even in these safe spaces with trained facilitators, the actual practice of talking about strong, complex, or what we have labeled as negative emotions is difficult. Talking about deep sadness, fear, grief, or emotional pain can feel too personal, too vulnerable, and too off-putting to share even in these supportive environments. Instead groups drift toward the safer topics about the latest treatments, healthy recipes, their various symptoms, and symptom management. A surprising number of support groups for people living with illness avoid any mention of the emotional toll illness can take. People share stories of courage, determination, hope, and overcoming the odds, but their other important stories of fear, anger, and despair rarely make it into open discussion.

Anne Goelitz, a social work clinician and researcher, has seen how easily support groups shy away from talking about strong negative emotions. In her research, she found mention of one such group that even went so far as to brush past the fact that one of their members had died. The grief was too strong and the fears too powerful; the group facilitators could not bring themselves to push the group into the deep emotional waters of coming to terms with death.[7] Without emotional sharing, these groups languish. They devolve into friendly chat sessions, which might seem like enough on the surface, but most often are not enough. Rather than finding a safe place in which they can acknowledge tough emotions, members instead find another polite space that has no room for their pain. People leave feeling even more isolated, convinced that their private emotions are too strong, too overwhelming even for these specialized spaces.

Goelitz is another clinician who recognized that dreams could help in her work. She began asking her clients about their dreams and found when they talked about a dream it helped them express the more distressing feelings they had been keeping hidden. None of these distressing feelings surprised anyone, but instead helped people come forward with their own pain. The dreams became a communication tool. They offered a less threatening mode of expressing complex emotions, making it easier for them to then explore the feelings out loud. Goelitz began introducing dream work into her support groups and found people gladly moving into a deeper mode of sharing very quickly. As she describes:

> I have found that dream work bypassed much of the focus on physical symptoms and treatment options, helping individuals talk about emotional issues instead. This reduced their feeling of being alone and

---

7. Ann Goelitz, "Dreaming Their Way into Life: A Group Experience with Oncology Patients," *Social Work With Groups* 24 (2002): 58.

allowed for frank talks about important issues including the proximity of death.[8]

The dream gave them just enough distance from their raw
emotions to help them acknowledge their fears, anger, and
grief, and other group members responded with their own
contradictory emotional responses to illness. As a result, the
groups became enlivened with new energy. It might seem a
bit of a paradox, but being able to talk about these deeper
emotions helped support group members feel bolder and
more alive. They felt stronger and more deeply connected to
the reality of their life.

Tallulah Lyons has been leading support groups focused
exclusively on dream work for people living with cancer since
2005. She found it didn't matter if the dreams were terrible or
uplifting, strong or confusing. Participants have consistently
reported enormous benefits from being part of these groups,
including experiencing less anxiety and stress, and more connection with others and with their own inner strengths. They
felt more confident and in control of their life, and better
able to live fully in the present.[9] The dreams opened them to
new energy and courage in their lives.

Help Us Talk about Dying

If talking about emotions at the end of life is difficult, talking
about dying—acknowledging out loud that we are approaching

8. Ann Goelitz, "Exploring Dream Work at End of Life," *Dreaming* 17
   (2007): 164.

9. Tallulah Lyons, *Dreams and Guided Imagery: Gifts for Transforming Illness
   and Crisis* (Bloomington, IN: Balboa Press, 2012), 243.

the end of life—is nearly impossible. Sometimes dreams can help people at the end of life acknowledge to their families the fact that they are dying.

Part of what makes facing death so difficult is all the success of modern medicine. We can now live well with diseases that once were considered a death sentence, so much so that we are surprised to learn some diseases still have no known cure. Rather than giving up, we now fight life-threatening illness with determination. We turn away from images of deathbeds and enter something resembling a battlefield. We hold in high esteem those people who battle illness, who survive on guts and willpower in the fight against death. We celebrate their strength, resilience, and determination. They didn't give up. Health care professionals encourage people to hold out hope for a cure, better treatment, or one more treatment that will help them live a little longer.

These messages of hope and strength are good, but they often come with a hidden cost. Many people have found it hard to know when exactly they should rally for a new fight and when they should say their goodbyes. Modern technology makes it hard to know when death is inevitable and when it is merely close, as in a close call, as in not now. What used to be valued as grace and dignity in bearing the inevitable end of life now looks to modern eyes like someone has given up and maybe given up too soon. Few people are ready to tell their families, "I am dying, and this is what I want for my funeral..." and few families are ready to ask. People who are ill don't want to distress their families by giving up. Families don't want to distress the person who is ill by noticing out loud they are failing.

They instead protect each other from the painful reality of death and in the process lose the chance to be each other's support and comfort. By protecting each other from their emotional pain, they lose sight of other important emotions that also emerge at the end of life, such as joy, laughter, hope, and peace, all of which could belong to them as well.

Just as dreams can help members of support groups bring up uncomfortable emotions, dreams can help people at the end of life bring up the topic of dying. A good dream can take as fearful a subject as death and fashion it into an emotionally resonant story that reassures our fears.

Jay Libby is a chaplain working in a major hospital in Boston.[10] He meets with people who are in the hospital for any number of reasons, but most often he meets with people who have exhausted all treatment options. Many have just found out they are dying. Libby rarely asks the people he visits about their dreams, but people will offer him their dreams anyway as one way they make sense out of their situation. He has seen how a dream can help people talk to each other in ways they weren't able to before. As Libby says, dreams help people say "the things we can't say, don't think we can say, not even sure we have to say, but somehow our dreams help us put them into words."

Libby once met an elderly woman (I will call her Marie), who was not doing well in the hospital. Her adult children had gathered and were trying to encourage her to eat when Libby arrived. Marie told him she wanted help talking to her family about a dream she'd had about her husband, long

---

10. Reverend Jay Libby, chaplain. All quotes from Jay are from my telephone interviews with him in September 2012 and July 2013.

since deceased. In Marie's dream, her husband had come for her. He reassured her that he was waiting for her. She explained to all of them it meant she could die in peace now, because she knew her husband was waiting for her. As Libby understood her, the dream "gave her the opportunity to verbalize with her family, 'I'm tired, I want to go back with Joe. He's waiting for me and he came by to tell me that.'"

Marie waited for the chaplain's visit to tell her dream to her family because she needed his support. She used her dream to help her family understand she was ready to die. Her dream gave her children permission to let her go as well. The dream reassured them they could stop pushing her to eat or asking the doctors for one more life-prolonging treatment. The dream gave them all permission to support her as she let go with dignity.

This story shows how well dreams can communicate our deepest emotions. Marie's dream helped her express her love for her children, her desire to see her husband again, and her sense that dying would bring her peace. Couched in the language of a dream, her deepest wish to die could be allowed, accepted, and cherished. I can imagine these children in five years' time looking back and telling each other again about her dream. My guess—my hope, really—is that the memory of this dream brings them a sense of peace and completeness. They won't have to worry they stopped fighting for her recovery too soon. They can know she felt held by her dream and that they had respected her wishes.

Dreams allow what might have once been unspeakable to be said out loud. There is less vulnerability in describing an objective image or event—even a dreamed one—than admitting to a powerful emotion. The images carry the emotions we can't yet find voice for. The dream of the elderly woman's husband welcoming her home was a more objective image than her bare emotions would have been and gave the woman and her family emotional room to say their goodbyes.

Dreams like this one help make the last days of a person's life rich and deeply satisfying. Instead of arguing over treatments, families can gather to remember together, talk about what is most important to them, and let their loved one go. They are relieved of much of the guilt that so often drags at families that maybe they haven't done enough, fought hard enough, or loved the person well enough to find the cure. A dream like this gives families a chance to simply be with the person, wishing her peace as she closes her eyes.

Monique Seguin, the licensed practical nurse in Quebec, has heard many dreams that help people begin what had been terrifying conversations for them. One woman admitted to Seguin's hospice unit refused to talk about dying even as she grew frailer. The hospice staff didn't need her to talk about dying, but they could see she was frightened, and they wished they knew of a way to reassure her. One evening Seguin asked her about dreams. And she said,

"Actually I had a dream this afternoon about you!" In her dream, she was walking with a little dog beside her, and she was not afraid. She was thinking, "I'm okay because Monique will know what to do with the dog." Because the dog needed to be tamed.

Seguin asked her what she thought it meant and she answered, "You know." Seguin asked her if she was afraid and at first she said no! But then she admitted she was afraid to die, and she was able to talk about it for the first time. After that conversation she felt much calmer, and she died peacefully a week later.

This woman's dream gave her one final chance to approach her fears and find help from the staff supporting her. I have no doubt she dreamed of Seguin because of Seguin's well-known interest in dreams at that hospice. The woman's dream image of a dog that needed taming helped her understand her fears could be tamed as well. Her dream gave her hope for some small resolution, and Seguin's invitation to talk about dreams was the last bit of permission she needed.

I have met many kind and loving families who want nothing more than to protect their loved ones from the harsh reality of death and loss. They hold their own grief in silence because they don't want to upset their families with their emotions. What they don't often realize is their loved one is doing the same thing—protecting them from their own strong emotions. I have no doubt they love each other. I can see them working hard to respect each other's wishes. But too often families are guessing what their loved ones might be thinking, and too often they guess what their loved one most wants is avoidance. They protect each other from the grim truth and, as a result, they each feel alone. They each wind themselves into emotional isolation right up until the last days. They have made emotional silos for themselves out of their love for each other.

If this sounds like your family, know that you are not alone. Nearly all families go through a time of strained communication as individuals try to figure out how much they can say without causing distress.

The consequences of all this misguided, loving protection is a missed opportunity for true intimacy when such intimacy is needed most. If nobody talks about dying, it makes it that much more difficult to talk about what really matters at the end of life. How can you say goodbye to someone when you can't acknowledge he or she is leaving?

There is so much to say at the end of life. Spouses and children can remember together what went right, what they have forgiven, what they will remember, what important lessons they will carry forward into the next generation. The person who is dying can give last words and tell again the stories about grandparents, great-grandparents, and what life was like for the family. All of these conversations become possible if the people involved find a way to break their protective silence.

In hospice care, nurses, social workers, doctors, and chaplains will all offer ways to open these conversations. We ask, "What is happening with you these days?" We get more observant and say, "I notice you're losing weight and seem less energetic." We invite them to say out loud what they see and feel, and we ask, "What do you think is happening here? Have you talked with each other about what you want?" The questions are gentle invitations into a new conversation about the reality they face.

The conversations of farewell are not easy. Most of us will worry about what to say and when to say it. Sometimes we do need to give our reassurance that we will be all right, but few of us know exactly when the right moment is for that conversation. How do we acknowledge the inevitable when we still want and need hope? What if we make our tearful, most heartfelt goodbyes and then they linger on? Will we survive our embarrassment if we say goodbye too soon?

Clinical hypnotherapist and spiritual counselor Mary Anne Sanders writes movingly of her mother's final illness in her book, *Nearing Death Awareness*. She also recounts her own stumbling attempt to enter a real conversation before her mother died. Soon after her mother was admitted to a residential hospice, her mother began talking about moving, which Sanders recognized as typical symbolic language about dying. As Sanders describes, one day her mother "angrily informed me that she was being moved to another bed upstairs (the hospice was a one-floor building). When I asked her why she was being moved, she replied, 'I don't know, but I don't like it one bit!'" [11]

Still, Sanders and her aunt both summoned up the courage to give her mother their permission to let go, to which her mother replied tartly, "I don't think I'm as sick as you think I am." To everyone's surprise except her mother's, her mother's health did improve, her confusion lessened, and she stopped talking of moving. And Sanders stopped talking about letting her go.

I have to believe Sanders didn't regret for a minute that she got herself ready for her mother's death or that she encouraged her mother, out loud, to let go. Her words drew

---

11. Mary Anne Sanders, *Nearing Death Awareness: A Guide to the Language, Visions, and Dreams of the Dying* (London: Jessica Kingsley, 2007), 30–31.

her closer to her mother and gave them a chance to talk again about the separation that was still looming. Their conversations gave them another chance to say something real, and her mother gave Sanders permission to use this story in her book.

The courage to say something true at such a tender moment is worth the embarrassment of maybe being wrong. We have done what feels impossible. We have readied ourselves to let go and opened a vulnerable place in our hearts. If our timing is off, we may have to apologize for thinking they are worse off than they are, as Sanders surely did. We may have to regroup emotionally and allow ourselves to reconnect and hold them close even as we know we will have to say goodbye again. But all that is doable. All that is forgivable.

Dreams can help invite these conversations. I have found the simple question—*How are your dreams these days?*— sometimes is all that is needed to give the dying person room to talk about their death. Just one dream told to friends or family can help all involved draw closer to each other.

I remember one man answering my question about dreams by describing a dream that transformed his relationships with his wife and children before my eyes. Before I met him, his wife informed me he had been stoically enduring his illness for more than a year by not talking about it. His family looked anxious and drawn when I arrived. Two daughters, one son, one son-in-law, and three teenage grandchildren all arranged themselves about his hospital bed in the living room, and no one spoke. The man himself was lying back in the bed with his eyes closed, and he didn't acknowledge me when I sat down and introduced myself. When I asked him how he was feeling, he nodded his head once.

I paused a moment in the heavy silence, then I asked, "How are your dreams these days?" His eyes snapped open, and he stared at me. I heard someone behind me gasp. He pushed himself up a little straighter and said calmly, "I had an interesting dream a few nights ago."

All these years later, I can't remember a single detail of his dream. But I am still taken by how quickly the emotional temperature of the room changed. His children leaned forward, nodding and smiling as he spoke, and two began tearing up. When he was finished, his wife moved to sit on the bed with him and took one of his hands and kissed it.

I asked him what he thought about the dream, and he shrugged without comment. His youngest daughter began laughing through her tears, and I knew whatever message he was sending had been received. I thanked him for telling the dream and then moved aside to let his family surge forward, many of them now talking quickly, laughing, and crying. After a while I needed to gently turn them back to the mundane task I had come to do, but now each person in the room looked lighter and more settled. There was general laughter and appreciation of each other.

This man used my invitation to open a much-needed conversation with his family, which gave them all a chance to talk together. I didn't offer any interpretation of my own or push him to think more deeply about the dream; it was clear he was telling the dream to his family. Over the next three weeks they talked often. They reflected on his life, shared memories, made their amends, and eventually they said their goodbyes. His one dream made all of those conversations possible. When he shared his dream, he gave them all permission to talk openly, which they gratefully accepted.

Not all dreams lead to such dramatic conversations among family members as this one did, but I believe all dreams carry this potential for a more open conversation. The dream work of support groups has shown the powerful connections people find when they share dreams, regardless of what the dreams are about. The act of telling a dream builds trust and emotional safety between dreamers and listeners, and this helps people live fully right up to the end.

Chapter Summary

Dreams are designed for helping us talk to people we trust about what is most important in our lives, whether it's our job, our health, our past, or our deepest beliefs. Each dream is a jumping-off point—a short tale that can lead us out of the polite talk of weather and into our most pressing concerns. Dreams help us talk about strong emotions, their images and plots often riding along a current of love, pain, or fear that can be understood better when we speak the dreams out loud. At the end of life, dreams can help us open the most difficult conversations we will ever face, the conversations about dying, death, loss, and how we will grieve. They allow what might have been unspeakable to be said aloud, and this sharing—this subtle opening of vulnerability—can help make the last days richer and more meaningful.

Talking about Dreams

- Have you ever wished you could talk to someone you love more openly about the end of life? What held you back? What do you think could have helped?

- Have you ever started a difficult conversation by telling a story? What happened? How would using a dream change the conversation?

- As with anything in life, using dreams to talk about daily life takes practice. How could you begin practicing now with the people you love?

Chapter Three

Preparation Dreams
Help Us Get Ready

Dreams about death are fairly common throughout our lives. Most people remember a few dreams in which they fight off threats, witness destruction, or run away from monsters. The common dream of falling is filled with the fear of death at the end of the fall. Dream researchers know most dreams about death are powerful symbols for how we are feeling in our daily life. Kelly Bulkeley and Patricia Bulkley, the authors of *Dreaming Beyond Death: A Guide to Pre-Death Dreams and Visions,* note that death images in dreams can be metaphors for all kinds of change, such as maturation and the death of childhood.[12] People will dream of being in mortal danger more often and more vividly when they are under stress. Survivors of accidents, wars, fires, and floods will often dream of catastrophes to sort through the strong emotions such losses bring.

At the end of life, however, when death itself becomes a very real threat, our dreams shift focus. When death moves

---

12. Kelly Bulkeley and Patricia Bulkley, *Dreaming Beyond Death: A Guide to Pre-Death Dreams and Visions* (Boston: Beacon Press, 2005).

from being just another metaphor for change and becomes a reality instead, our dreams surprisingly become more comforting and more hopeful. As we come closer to death, our dreams begin helping us prepare for the moment of letting go.

Psychiatrist and Jungian analyst Marie-Louise von Franz learned from her clinical work that end-of-life dreams carry two important messages to the dreamer. The first is the calm, direct, occasionally visceral assertion that the body will die. In these dreams, things break down, doctors walk away shaking their heads, the dreamer hears there is nothing more to be done, or a voice tells them flat out that they are dying. Some dreams use gruesome images of rotting and decaying flesh to make their point.

The second message is equally clear and confident: the dreamer—the soul, the personality, the spirit—will doubtless continue to live on past the body's death. As von Franz understands it, our unconscious, dreaming self does not recognize physical death as the end of us as individuals. More often (much more often), our dreams show death as another stage of personal growth and development. They don't depict images of hitting a wall of nothingness or personal annihilation. Instead they show the dreamer traveling to a new place, meeting old and cherished friends again, and finding help and comfort from someplace beyond physical life.[13] For von Franz, dying dreams bring comfort and a healing of the soul.

---

13. Marie-Louise von Franz, *On Dreams & Death* (Boston: Shambhala, 1986): viii–ix. "In cases where the dreamer has illusions about his approaching death or is unaware of its closeness, dreams may…indicate this fact quite brutally and mercilessly." "The unconscious psyche pays very little attention to the abrupt end of bodily life and behaves as if the psychic life of the individual…will simply continue."

Other clinicians who have written about end-of-life dreams report the same observation. As people draw closer to death, their dreams become progressively more comforting and more reassuring. Our dreams stop amplifying our negative emotional states and instead begin offering hope and comfort.

Jungian analyst Mark Welman provides a good example of what this dream progression looks like. For his doctoral dissertation he interviewed Peter, a seventy-one-year-old retired engineer "who recalled dreams infrequently and had little interest in psychology, mythology, or related issues" before agreeing to take part in Welman's study about dreams at the end of life.[14] Peter told Welman a total of seven dreams over the next six months. I've included three here—his first, fourth, and last dream from the study—to show how dreams can progress from messages of impending doom to messages of hope and comfort.

- *Dream 1: I dreamed I had two bodies, which fitted together like two parts of something. ... One body was slowly lifting out of and floating away from the other one.*

- *Dream 4: I was a computer which wasn't working. Somebody called the technicians who said that there was something wrong with my part and that they would have to get new parts to put into me. ... But when they looked they couldn't find any spare parts.*

---

14. Mark Welman, *Death and Gnosis: Archetypal Dream Imagery in Terminal Illness,* (South Africa: Rhodes University, 1996), 255. Retrieved January 9, 2013, http://eprints.ru.ac.za/1769/. Used with permission.

- *Dream 7 (final dream): I dreamed of a bright flower. ... I thought that I had always wanted one like that in my garden.*[15]

The day Peter told his seventh and final dream, he surprised the researchers by formally shaking their hands and wishing them luck in all future research. He had begun the research project feeling angry and depressed; now he appeared not only relaxed but serene. He died a few days later.

Peter's first and fourth dreams showed his impending sense of loss. In the first he was quite literally losing his body, and in the fourth he saw himself as a computer that was broken beyond repair. The final dream did not offer him the comfort of angels or guides, something he didn't believe in. Instead he saw a beautiful flower he had always wanted, and the image helped him find peace.

The question has remained open as to how common it is for dreams to shift into a comforting mode at the end of life. Did Peter's dreams change because he was dying and that's what dreams do, or did they change because he was Peter and that is what he needed? Dream researchers, like the people who talked with Peter, have often limited their studies to the dreams of a very few clients, sometimes only one. Researchers who have attempted to gather more end-of-life dreams often shied away from asking the people who are dying directly. They worried about imposing upon people at such a fragile time and instead relied on caregivers, families, and nursing staff to recount dreams that had been offered by patients to them. These dreams were often selected and remembered because they were emotionally significant, which

---

15. Ibid., Appendix B.

doesn't answer the question of how common such comforting dreams can be.

In the past few years, the Center for Hospice and Palliative Care in Buffalo, New York, has begun groundbreaking research on end-of-life dreaming. Their first important discovery was that many people who entered into hospice care were willing to share their dreams. Some welcomed a chance to make a lasting contribution, but most wanted the emotional support of having someone listen to their dreams. They wanted help in exploring their dreams.[16]

In one study the hospice research team followed sixty-three inpatient hospice residents every day over an eighteen-month period, or until the participants were no longer able to talk. They were all mentally clear, and none were taking medications that might induce hallucinations. All in all, the researchers gathered reports of 269 dreams or visions. An astounding 88 percent of these people were able to remember and describe at least one dream or waking vision at the end of their lives. The team's first published study confirms what clinicians have observed in their work with individuals for the past several decades. People continue to dream throughout their lives. Those dreams often bring comfort and hope, becoming more direct and more apparent as death approaches, and help the dreamers prepare emotionally for the end of life. The researchers conclude,

> A person's fear of death often diminishes as a direct result [of the dreams]... and what arises is a new insight

---

16. Pei Grant, researcher with the Center for Hospice and Palliative Care, personal communication, January 2014.

into mortality. The emotional impact is ... comforting and paradoxically life affirming; the individual is physically dying, but their emotional and spiritual identity remains present ... [The dreams] do not deny death, but in fact, transcend the dying experience.[17]

At their deepest level, dreams at the end of life underline an assumption that we are more than our physical bodies and that who we are transcends if not our physical death, then certainly our dying. Our dreams view dying as the next great emotional and spiritual challenge to face and accept.

I have seen these preparation dreams help many people at the end of life in my own work. Preparation dreams remind dreamers of what is most important in their lives and of what they still want to accomplish. Dreams of journeys help people move forward into a new, safe place or embark on a new adventure. Dreams can help dreamers gather their emotional strength when physical strength is failing. Dreamers meet old friends and deceased loved ones who are waiting and begin to imagine an existence beyond their death.

Dreams can do all this because they are always coming from our deepest wishes and best intentions for ourselves. Our dreams come for our benefit alone and can help us better understand what we want and need most. By listening to our dreams, we rediscover the meaning our life has for us right now, which connects us again to our hopes.

---

17. Christopher W. Kerr, James P. Donnelly, Scott T. Wright, Sarah M. Kuszczak, Anne Banas, Pei C. Grant, and Debra L. Luczkiewicz, "End-of-Life Dreams and Visions: A Longitudinal Study of Hospice Patients' Experiences," *Journal of Palliative Medicine* (January 2014): 12.

Help Us Finish the Business of Life

There is so much ending at the end of a life. It is a daily, sometimes hourly, procession of losses and goodbyes. Every day brings a new physical frailty and another small, potent ending. People nearing the end of life hang up the phone after talking to a friend and wonder if that was their last conversation. They stumble as they take out the trash and know someone else will have to do this from now on. They sit in a wheelchair for the first time and wonder if they will ever stand again. Each change reminds them that everything they have ever known will end, in fact is ending a bit at a time—first their work and hobbies, and eventually their strength, balance, and endurance.

Dreams help put the emotional experience of loss into a manageable, physical form. In dreams people put their homes in order, shutter the windows, pack their clothes, and put precious things away. Some will dream of setting their affairs in order and wake up with renewed determination to do the same in daily life.

These dreams can be distressing reminders of what is yet left unfinished, or they can express our emotions in a more symbolic form. One man had several anxiety dreams, including one in which his work colleagues were trying to kidnap him.[18] When he woke, he knew his colleagues meant him no harm. He saw the dream as an expression of his anxiety that something was left undone. A mother of young children was

---

18. Cheryl L. Nosek, Christopher W. Kerr, Julie Woodworth, Scott T. Wright, Pei C. Grant, Sarah M. Kuszczak, Anne Banas, Debra L. Luczkiewicz, and Rachel M. Depner, "End of Life Dreams and Visions: A Qualitative Perspective from Hospice Patients," *American Journal of Hospice and Palliative Care* (January 2014): 9–10.

distressed by dreams in which she was "getting her children ready for school, getting them to practices." [19] The dream reminded her of what was still left to do in her life and of the pain she felt about leaving her children.

These dreams can lead to much-needed conversations about what is still left undone and what still needs to be accomplished before the dreamer feels ready to let go. The dream opens a delicate conversation of what worries continue to nag at the person who is dying, including handling unpaid bills, settling funeral plans, and making sure family left behind will be all right. Dreams can urge people to pass along their knowledge to their family or reassure the dreamer their spouse can learn how to cook, look after the car, and pay the mortgage.

Telling the dream gives everyone a chance to know better what the dreamer thinks still needs doing, mending, or holding before they die. Listening without adding an interpretation allows the dreamer to decide if the dream is using symbolic language to express emotion or if it is directing the patient to take care of something specific.

When the dreamer tells a dream, it gives new importance to both the dream and the dreamer. It tells everyone that what the dreamer thinks and feels is still important. It may seem obvious that the dreamer is still important, but when physical care needs mount up it's easy for a person to wonder if they have already taken up too much of the caregiver's time and support. The dream puts the dreamer, and not just the dreamer's body, back into the conversation.

---

19. Ibid., 10.

Help Us Gather Our Strength

Preparation dreams can also remind us of our inner strength to meet the last, greatest unknown. In *Dreaming Beyond Death,* Patricia Bulkley recounts her meeting with Bill, a retired merchant marine ship's captain, who fell into a depression after hearing from his doctor that he was going to die soon. Bill withdrew from his family and everything he had once considered important. After some coaxing he agreed to be seen by Bulkley, who was working then as a hospice chaplain. She visited him at his home, where he showed her mementos from his life at sea. She found a Bible verse that encouraged him to take heart.[20]

When Bulkley came back to see him a few days later, she noticed a profound change in his emotional well-being. He greeted Bulkley with a warm smile. She could see a renewed vitality about him, even in his illness. Bill explained he had been remembering how he used to read Bible passages when he was out at sea, standing at the helm and looking out over the ocean, knowing God was with him, "even though we weren't always sure exactly where 'there' was in those days." And then he had this dream:

> *I am sailing again at night in uncharted waters and the old sense of adventure comes back. I feel the tingle of excitement again, of pushing through the waves in the vast, dark, empty sea but knowing somehow I am right on course. And strangely enough, I'm not afraid to die anymore. In fact, I feel ready to go, more so every day.*[21]

---

20. Bulkeley and Bulkley, *Dreaming Beyond Death*, 1.

21. Ibid., 3.

To many of us death can feel like a vast, dark emptiness—uncharted, unknown, and so much greater in scope than our fragile lives. This man's dreams did not lessen the vastness of death or how much was still unknown to him. The dream didn't tame the waves or create a pretty rainbow. The dream did not take away his recognition of death as out of his control and uncharted or dark and empty.

Instead, his dream reminded him that he already knew how to face such an immense event with courage and a wild joy. It reminded him that he could sail into the dark and emerge safely, that he could trust his own ability to ride out the waves. It reminded him that such dark unknown vastness was part of the allure for him of sailing. It recalled in him a deep thrill, both a sense of adventure and a deep trust in something greater than him. In the dream he was reminded of his assurance that God was with him even when facing an entity so much larger than his own life.

He woke up with his fear lessened, not because death was now smaller, but because he remembered his own courage when sailing through the perilous sea. He didn't need to figure out what else his sailing dream might mean. Its message was clear and bold, and it spoke directly to his fears and his strengths. Even though he knew he could never control the waves or the darkness, he woke with the reassurance that his dying might be as peaceful and ultimately as safe as his earlier sea voyages.

Bulkley's Bible verses might have stirred the merchant marine captain's imagination enough for him to find his dream, but without that dream would he have remembered so clearly what it felt like to be in danger and trusting at the same time? Only the dream of sailing blind through a dark ocean—something he remembered—could bring such a visceral experience of meeting death with trust and courage.

In their book *Dreams and Death: The Benefits of Dreams Before, During, and After Death*, Nicole Gratton and Monique Seguin describe a young man who was dying of lung cancer. Before he came into hospice, he had fought hard to keep himself alive, running after every new treatment until nothing more could be done.[22] In his early dreams he was also always running after something, never catching up, and always painfully short of breath. In his eyes these dreams reflected both his determination to live and his fears that no matter how hard he tried, health was just beyond his reach. Now his running dream took on a new form. The small shift made a huge difference.

> *I see myself running in a place where everything is beautiful. It is very pleasant because I am not short of breath. I run easily, and I'm having fun.*[23]

This last dream reflects his acceptance of the end of his life, something that his family and caregivers had all noticed. In this dream he had his strength and purpose back. Now he could see the beauty of the place in which he ran. Now he had a blissful acceptance that gave him and his family time to love and appreciate each other in his final days. His life became beautiful and full of a new purpose—to love his family and be loved and cherished in return.

---

22. Gratton and Seguin, *Dreams and Death*, 27.
23. Ibid.

Sometimes dreams bring images of movement that are so tiny it is hard to imagine they bring the same comfort, but they are no less significant. Marie-Louise von Franz cites a young psychologist's thesis when she tells of Suzanne, an elderly woman who was in the final days of a long illness and remained terrified of death.[24] Then she had a dream of a small candle burning brightly on her hospital room's windowsill. As she watched, the candle suddenly went out, leaving her in darkness. Before she could panic the light reappeared, now just outside the window. The candle had moved only a few inches from just inside the hospital room to just beyond the window, but she took enormous comfort in watching that candle burning just as brightly and surely as ever, out in the dark beyond the safety of her known world. She knew from that dream that her life somehow would also continue. She was going to be like the flame, going out in physical life only to light up again on the other side. The next morning she told her doctor she was ready to die.

It was such a small movement but so significant. The candle flame was like her life, small and fluttering against the cold window with only darkness outside. When the candle relit itself outside the window, steady and clear, it told her all she needed to know about the next world. The candle survived the move—just as she would survive.

Dreams such as these turn our attention away from the helplessness of the body and back toward the fearlessness of our spirit. If dying is like embarking on a journey, then a journey needs our consent, our action, our courage, and our

---

24. Millie Kelly Fortier, "Dreams and Preparation for Death," *ProQuest Dissertations and Theses* (1972): 1. Retrieved March 20, 2014.

daring as we steer our ship on the open ocean or as we set out on a run or as we follow our spirit in the fluttering of a candle.

The power of these dreams lies in the images themselves. The dreamers didn't have to tell anyone else to feel reassured by them. The dreams spoke directly to their greatest fears and gave them a way to resolve those fears. They also didn't need to hear that these dreams might be symbolic messages about death or dying. If they never consciously thought of the dreams as helping them die, they still received enormous comfort from them. The dreams themselves were enough.

By listening without interpretation, we help the dreamer hold on to the images. Telling the dream to others strengthens the images in the dreamer's minds, strengthens the dream's effect on them, and validates their trust in the dream's importance. The dreams offer their own comfort without our interpretations or questions.

Set Us on a Journey

I met Sylvie through our church when she was reaching the end of her life. Sylvie was a strong-willed woman whose force of character more than made up for her tiny and frail physical frame. She had not been able to get out of her wheelchair for several years and needed help with everything, but she had a sharp mind. Rather than define herself by her disability, she considered herself a trainer of her young caregivers to meet her needs. Her piercing gaze gave me the impression of a hawk, but she loved making silly, over-the-top expressions of shock, amusement, mock anger, and confusion—whatever could make me laugh. I visited her every two weeks to give her news of our church and read poems and prayers.

We didn't talk about dreams until one day when she reported she had been busy packing all week. I glanced around her immaculate apartment. Over by the kitchenette her caregiver silently shook her head no, and I realized Sylvie had most likely been dreaming of moving.

If Sylvie had told me this was a dream, I might have asked her what it reminded her of and how she made sense of it. But she talked about it like it was a real event. She had always liked travel, and in her younger days she had lived in several different countries for her family's business. Now she looked satisfied and excited by the prospect of pulling up stakes. Her life had become interesting again, and I wanted her to hold on to that. So I asked her how the packing was coming along.

"Moving is hard work," she said. "I've been moving for two weeks now, and I'm tired."

"Where are you moving to?" I asked, and she gestured vaguely with her good hand toward the window. "Over there, on the other side of the lakeside, the beach. Next door. I mean, out there."

She greeted me with the same story for the next three visits. She was moving, getting ready to move, packing her things up. Once, she was so convinced the move would take place in the next few days that I surreptitiously asked the caregiver again on my way out the door. The caregiver shook her head. "No, she's not moving anywhere. I don't know why she tells you that."

Sylvie *was* moving. She was growing weaker and more confused. I could see dramatic physical changes. Each visit she slumped farther down in her wheelchair. She took longer to eat and slept more. Her hands rested more often in her lap. I continued to read her poems as her responses dwindled to a smile or a grimace, nodding to ask me to read some of them again. Our conversations grew more disjointed as she struggled to make sense of what was happening to her.

Then one day Sylvie greeted me with an energy I hadn't seen for months. She sat up straight in her chair, laughing a bit with her caregiver. She waved me over and informed me she had just come back from a marvelous cruise and was feeling refreshed, even though she had danced quite a bit. Behind her the caregiver rolled her eyes. I sat down at the table and leaned forward. I said, "Tell me about it."

She described the ship as elegant in a modern, mid-century style. Nearly every passenger had his or her own private cruise director. The cruise ship had an orchestra and served "decent champagne" and upscale food. I was curious if Sylvie was seeing this dream as a symbolic movement for her, perhaps a preparation for her dying, but Sylvie stayed with the dream as a real memory. Rather than look for metaphors, I kept my attention focused on Sylvie's story.

Sylvie continued, "Everyone had a cruise director to guide them across and then help them ashore when they finally reached the other side."

I asked, "Did you go ashore when you reached the other side, too?"

"No, of course not! I came back with the crew."

"Why not stay?"

She glared at me in mock anger. "Well, for some strange reason no one has yet explained to me, I was assigned a new tour director—a student—and I had to train her. She hadn't learned enough by the time we reached the other side, so I came back with them."

"Oh well," I said, "maybe the next cruise she will have more experience."

Sylvie looked hopeful. "Will there be another cruise?"

"I don't know why there wouldn't be," I said, "especially if you've taken the trouble to train this director. I would hope you'd get a chance to see her at her best."

Sylvie smiled and said, "I would like that."

Our conversation about Sylvie's dream lasted just under twenty minutes. It was the most coherent conversation we'd had in several months and, as it turned out, it was the last coherent conversation we had together. Over the next week her health declined rapidly. And then she died, peacefully, with her family around her.

Sylvie's dream cruise shows again how little interpretation is needed for a dream at the end of life to bring comfort. Like Daniel in chapter 2, who went out dancing in his dreams and brought home the tales to his family, Sylvie didn't need to understand it was a dream at all. She felt her life brighten from the exhilaration of her adventure. She felt secure enough to look forward to future travels, and I hope in her final hours she did find another ship waiting for her.

Dreams of journeys and traveling can occur at any point in life. They are most common when people are facing major transitions such as changing jobs, graduating, marrying or divorcing, or having children, to name a few. At the end of life, however, journey and travel dreams become more common and take on a new emotional resonance.

Fifty-nine percent of the people interviewed in the Center for Hospice and Palliative Care study had dreams about going somewhere in the last weeks of their life. Journey dreams like Sylvie's are so common in the last few days and weeks of life that health care workers often use them as one marker of approaching death.

In their dreams people pack for travel, close up shop, and wait in line. They buy cars, cross bridges, and board trains, ships, and airplanes. Their dream landscapes fill with airports and train stations and windows and doors. They cross oceans, walk down passageways, and step over thresholds into a place still unseen.

- *I stand alone on the shore of a lake. I decide to swim across it. To my great surprise, I realize I can swim. I feel wonderful. I reach the other side easily.*[25]
- *I know we are going somewhere, but I don't know where.*[26]
- *I can see the light down the road and it's beautiful.*[27]
- *I am leaving for Florida with my friend Jeannine. I sing all the way. We are traveling in a Winnebago. ... I was happy, happy, I was singing all the way!*[28]

---

25. Gratton and Seguin, *Dreams and Death*, 24.

26. Nosek, et al., "End of Life Dreams and Visions: A Qualitative Perspective from Hospice Patients," 8.

27. Maggie Callanan and Patricia Kelley, *Final Gifts: Understanding the Special Awareness, Needs, and Communications of the Dying* (New York: Bantam, 1997), 101.

28. Gratton and Seguin, *Dreams and Death*, 31.

These dreams are full of movement and a sense of safety, sometimes for the first time. The woman who swam easily across the lake remarked on it because she had always been afraid of the water and had never learned to swim. Now she swam easily to the other side, and when she woke, she found her fear of water and her fear of death had both disappeared. The dreams bring a comforting safety, and fears of the unknown rest easy. There is peace in the dream, along with a manageable adventure and sometimes excellent service. The dreamers wake with a newfound courage and hope.

Journey dreams can carry us through the most difficult parts of dying—past the gates we would never dare cross in waking life. They help us practice taking the next great step into the unknown by reminding us that we already know how to travel. Our dreams tell us this immense and unfathomable event may have more in common with the more mundane practice of moving to a new apartment or boarding a boat. In our dreams we take our leave, unmoor our hearts, and set sail. We practice saying goodbye to friends we leave behind on the shore. We practice letting go of our familiar place and stepping forward in trust.

Sylvie's dream of an elegant cruise gave her a measure of peace and reassurance that no words of mine could ever match. She had a night of pure enjoyment with dancing, classy food, better-than-average champagne, and good company. She came back refreshed and relaxed with a renewed hunger for traveling again—something she hadn't been able to do in more than two decades. Her dream gave her a future she could anticipate with pleasure, one that built on her strengths.

In her dream she also held on to her personal dignity by casting herself once again as a trainer, this time of a young cruise director. She defined herself by what she could still give—advice, direction, instruction—and not by her disability. Her choice to return when the others disembarked on the far side reminded her of her power, much like the power felt by the merchant marine captain who sailed the high seas.

Sylvie didn't need any extra interpretations for her dream, and I didn't explain to her about how end-of-life dreams can help. Instead my questions allowed the dream's pleasures and reassurances to resonate into her waking life. I gave Sylvie room to explore her reasons for going and then returning, and helped her anticipate a second voyage. She had a right to say as much or as little about her experience as she pleased and to set the pace for everything we talked about. It was her dream, her interpretation, her response, and her memory. She needed nothing more or less than a willing listener to help her bring the dream into her waking life.

Being allowed to tell her dream gave her the chance to re-live an important experience and revel in her adventure. She could bring the dream into her waking life more fully and experience it again with all the pleasure it had offered her the first time. Telling the dream became more than simply reminiscing; it helped anchor her experience more deeply in her mind and soul. It gave her the chance to bring me and her caregiver some startling news—that amidst the suffering of debility, the end of life also brings adventure, hope, challenge, and decent champagne.

Chapter Summary

Any dream can be a preparation dream, regardless of its images, if it helps us prepare for the ending of our lives. Dreams can remind us of what we still want or need to do. They help us gather our strength by reminding us of what keeps us strong inside, whether that is courage, curiosity, or faith. In some preparation dreams we pack up, get in line for a train or an airplane, or set out on a journey. We practice moving forward into our future with confidence and a deep assurance of our personal safety. Dreams like the one Sylvie had show another important aspect that is common in preparation dreams. She had a guide—in her instance a tour guide—to help her make the journey.

Talking about Dreams

- Have you known someone who began talking of traveling at the end of life?

- Has a dream ever nudged you to do something you had been putting off? What did you do?

- Would you feel comfortable with your loved ones reveling in a dream journey they consider real, or would you want to remind them they are not actually traveling?

- Do you think a dream of a journey at the end of life is a metaphor for the soul's journey? Why or why not?

Chapter Four

Visitation Dreams Bring Us Loving Company

Visitation dreams bring the comforting presence of loved ones who have died before and are now waiting to accompany the dreamer to a loving afterlife. These dreams are different from the dream Tallulah's father had in the introduction. Jerry woke from a dream about his wife and remembered their life together with new appreciation, but he didn't think she had visited him. A visitation dream brings the dreamer a visceral sense of the deceased loved ones' actual presence. The dying person might even be awake when she sees her loved ones in the room and, smiling, reaches out to greet them.

My friend Kathy sat with her mother through her mother's last days. Their relationship had been rocky through the years, but they had become close again by the time her mother was diagnosed with Alzheimer's disease. At the end of her mother's life, Kathy helped her moved to a long-term care facility and visited her nearly every day. In the final days her mother drifted in and out of consciousness, not eating and not responding to anyone. It had been months since she had recognized anyone in her family, including Kathy. One afternoon Kathy was alone with her, talking softly to her in the hopes that her mother took comfort from the sound of her voice, when suddenly her mother opened her eyes and sat up a little bit. Kathy said it looked like a light had switched on in her mother's eyes.

> *There was a moment when she had total clarity. She looked out the window and she lifted up her head and she was smiling. For her to sit up in the bed like that was totally out of character. Her face was—it was glowing. Radiant. I said, "Mom, what do you see?" And she said, "Oh, Mamma and Poppa are coming to take me home!" And her face was just amazingly alive and alert in that moment. It was just incredible. I knew it was something that was beyond earthly stuff. I know that in her mind's eye they were real to her, and I totally believe that. It was just a very loving moment.*

After years of slowly fading into the darkness and confusion of Alzheimer's disease, Kathy's mother suddenly woke up clear-eyed and so much like her old self that Kathy was startled. In that one minute Kathy's mom looked radiant, glowing, happy, calm, and ready to be taken home. Kathy could tell her mother was seeing people she loved and trusted, and who loved her and were waiting for her. She could see in that moment her mother felt cared for, protected, encouraged, and safe. Kathy's mom couldn't say all this, but her expression spoke volumes. In that moment, she was herself again, her eyes bright and self-aware.

Kathy's mother had what I call a visitation dream. She wasn't awake in the hours leading up to this moment; she had been drifting in and out of a muddled consciousness for days. She wasn't exactly asleep, either; in that one moment she was alert and responsive to what she was seeing in the room with her. To Kathy's eyes, her mother's parents seemed less like a dream than a visit from people her mother trusted.

End-of-life conversations with deceased visitors often bring people's minds back to such a clear focus that they startle family and staff alike. Many people who have not spoken a word or opened their eyes for days will suddenly smile broadly and sit up, reach out their arms to welcome invisible beings, or speak to their deceased loved ones with their eyes clear and bright again.

Talk to any long-term care staff and you will find stories of such unusual one-sided conversations. It is not uncommon for them to walk into a patient's room and find that person speaking with or watching people they themselves can't see. Some patients might speak of the vivid presence of people they love who are right there in the room, giving messages of love and encouragement. The visitors sit on the end of the dying person's bed, lean against the door, lounge in the extra chair, and smile while the person is awake and talking to family. Some people will have long conversations with their visitors; others will simply mention casually to their family that Grandma is now sitting in the chair by the window.

Research suggests these visitation dreams are much more common than previously thought. Noted dream scholar Kelly Bulkeley and chaplain Patricia Bulkley report dreams such as these have been shared by dying people in every culture throughout human history.[29] The latest research from the Center for Hospice and Palliative Care in Buffalo found a full 72 percent of those who remembered their dreams had a dream of a deceased loved one who visited them.[30] Some of these dreams occurred months before they died, and some within a day or two. As with preparation dreams, visitation dreams become more frequent and more comforting as a person draws nearer to death.

Mary Anne Sanders gathered several examples from nursing home staff who witnessed both family members and patients reaching out with joy and acceptance.

- *One resident (at the home) was looking up toward the ceiling, smiling, holding out her hand, then saying, "There you are, I've been waiting for you."*
- *My husband's uncle, a minister, heard the angels singing. He said, "Just listen, they're singing beautifully."*
- *I've seen patients staring into the air and reaching out, calling the names of loved ones who were already dead.*[31]

In my early years as a hospital social worker, I walked in on enough of these moments to feel their emotional power. I would enter a person's hospital room feeling confident in my professional role only to see the patient reluctantly turn her eyes away from the ceiling or window or empty chair to

---

29. Bulkeley and Bulkley, *Dreaming Beyond Death*, 11.
30. Kerr, et al., "End-of-Life Dreams and Visions: A Longitudinal Study of Hospice Patients' Experiences," 9.
31. Sanders, *Nearing Death Awareness*, 45.

focus on me—polite but distant, as if I had just interrupted something beyond my comprehension.

Sometimes I asked people what they were seeing but most often they smiled without answering. I was a stranger to them, someone they would meet only once about the single topic of how to get them home safely. I didn't know them or their visitors, and most held on to these moments as their own. I wondered how many of these invisible visitations happened in hospitals every day, tucked carefully in between the visits of the various hospital staff and noticed only by the patients and the people they trusted enough to tell.

Visitation dreams, much like all dreams, are deeply entwined with the dreamer's life and values. The visitors carry a personal significance that goes beyond being merely a familiar figure—they are most often loved ones who brought the promise of comfort when they were alive, such as deceased parents and spouses or old friends. Only the person who is dying sees the familiar face of someone long dead and reaches out for him or her. Occasionally family members will feel a presence in the room, but most often they can only shake their heads in wonder.

Visitation dreams are marked by four characteristics: their vivid sense of realness, their comforting presence, the guidance they often offer, and the questions they raise about the afterlife.

Realness

The power of visitation dreams lies in the dreamer's recognition of the dream figures as true visitors. For the most part people don't wake up from visitation dreams and remark, "I dreamed about my mother and it reminded me of her care." People wake up from visitation dreams and say, "My mother came for me, my mother is waiting for me." The dreamer may have had many other dreams about her mother, but in this instance the dream no longer acts like a story carrying a message. In a visitation dream, the dream is more like a bridge between this world and the next, where loved ones are waiting. It's a powerful moment of hope, trust, and faith.

The vivid sense of objective realness of visitation dreams goes well beyond the clarity of other dreams at the end of life. The merchant marine captain in chapter 3 woke from a vivid dream about sailing again in uncharted waters, and the dream helped him remember his strength and trust in a power greater than himself. It was an important dream that helped him come to accept his death, and he felt comforted by the images, but he still recognized the dream as a dream. The power of his dream lay in how the images reminded him of his own strength.

Visitation dreams carry a shock of recognition that the dreamer is in the presence of another person. My friend Kathy watched her mother lift herself up in her last days and call for her parents with such joy that Kathy knew it had to be real. She said, "I know that in her mind's eye they were real to her, and I totally believe that." That sense of the visitation being real, more than a dream or a memory, is what gave Kathy a powerful relief and comfort. The reality of her grandparents' presence gave her mother's last days new meaning and peace.

People like Jay Libby, the hospital chaplain in Boston, hesitate to call them dreams at all because clients describe the visitations like any other waking event, as objectively real as visits they receive from their living friends. Enough people have seen visitors while awake and clear minded to make the idea of it being "just a dream" seem ludicrous. They know they aren't dreaming.

The Center for Hospice and Palliative Care researchers found that 45 percent of these visitations actually appeared in vivid dreams while only 15 percent of the participants said they were awake at the time. Another 40 percent of the participants had more than one visitation experience, some while they were awake and some while they were sleeping.[32] Even more intriguing, a few dreams were powerful enough to cross the boundary between sleep and wakefulness. As the researchers noted, "Pre-death dreams were frequently so intense that the dream carried into wakefulness and the dying often experienced them as waking reality."[33]

They were awake. They were asleep. They were awake. For many the question of whether they were dreaming or awake at the time of the visitation didn't matter. Jay Libby noticed some of the people who spoke about their visitation dreams never made the distinction between the two. What mattered was knowing that someone had come for them.

This realness takes some people on a spiritual journey. Libby estimates half of his hospital referrals come from people who need help understanding a visitation dream. For people who don't believe their dead loved ones can return, such a visitation can bring confusion along with its

---

32. Kerr, et al., "End-of-Life Dreams and Visions: A Longitudinal Study of Hospice Patients' Experiences," 10.
33. Ibid.

warmth, leading people to new spiritual questions. Some are afraid to tell their families about the visits because they themselves don't understand how it is possible. They ask Libby if their illness is affecting their brains and if they have lost not only their physical health but their mental capacities as well. Most want his permission to accept the comfort these visits offer them.

Libby helps people accept their visitation dreams as a real experience that has a real impact on their lives. Then he steps back and encourages them to make their own sense of what it means for them. Their visitation dreams become a starting point into a much larger conversation about life and death and what they expect, hope, or fear will come next.

Practitioners in Western medicine traditionally have explained away these visitation dreams as hallucinations brought on by medication, the underlying illness, or a lack of oxygen that causes the brain to misfire. New research, however, is finding there are clear differences between hallucinations and visitation dreams.[34] Hallucinations are most often meaningless—the images have no emotional connection to the person's life. With hallucinations, people see such things as bugs crawling up the wall and small animals or young children running blindly through the room without interacting. Hallucinations don't bring comfort; they create confusion and distress in the person who sees them. The people feel less sure of themselves and more frightened by the world around them. In these cases medicine can help lessen the hallucinations.

---

34. Sue Brayne, Chris Farnham, and Peter Fenwick, "Deathbed Phenomena and Their Effect on a Palliative Care Team: A Pilot Study," *American Journal of Hospice and Palliative Care* 23 (2006): 17–24. Retrieved October 11, 2012, http://ajh.saagepub.com/content/23/1/17.

Visitation dreams, on the other hand, are saturated with meaning. The visitors are familiar and most often dear to the person who is dying. In the Center for Hospice and Palliative Care study, nearly half of the visitors in visitation dreams were close family members who had already died, and another 17 percent were close family members who were still living but not present.[35] As Michele Chaban describes, these visitors are "people they have loved. Everybody that was in their life would suddenly start to present themselves in terms of connectedness. Very seldom was it fear or terror-driven."

Comforting Presence

Visitation dream visitors wait with the dying person and provide comfort just with their presence. They welcome, they smile, and they wait patiently. They can bring a remarkable calm and peace. Their presence alone lessens anxiety and pain in the dreamers and tells them that they are not alone, as when Kathy's mother reached out for her own parents. She saw something that at its very least reminded her of a time when she was held and cherished. In her heart, however, Kathy knew her mother's experience went deeper than that. Her mother's visitors let her know she was held and cherished right then, in that moment, when she needed comfort the most.

Visitation dreams are deeply personal and meaningful. People who are dying don't receive visits from deceased strangers who have no interest in them. They see people they know, love, and trust. This loving welcome is so strongly infused in the experience that some hospice professionals look

---

35. Kerr, et al., "End-of-Life Dreams and Visions: A Longitudinal Study of Hospice Patients' Experiences," 7.

for it specifically, to know it is a true visitation dream. Fiona Martins, the palliative care nurse in Toronto, looks for that loving, meaningful presence to help her distinguish between a visitation dream and a medical hallucination. If a patient of hers sees someone who is not familiar, not loving, and not welcoming, Martins assesses the patient for hallucinations.

I think this overwhelming love and care is a remarkable facet of visitation dreams. The visitors in visitation dreams seem not just like themselves; they appear as their best selves, free of old habits, anxieties, and emotional limitations. They don't show up in pain, even if they died in pain. They aren't suffering or confused about where they are, and they don't need help from the dying person. They aren't lonely for the dying person or anxious to be going. They aren't hurt or angry or irritated at all the trouble. Regardless of what had transpired in their lives, they no longer hold old resentments. They don't remind the dying person of past arguments or pain from when they were alive or gloat about their superior knowledge of what is waiting for the dying person. Dying people don't see old enemies lurking about just waiting to pick up the fight once they are in the great beyond. If dreamers do see old enemies, those people are more likely to apologize and then offer their help.

As one researcher declared to me, at the end of life these experiences circle around the one powerful, driving force of love. Love in its purest, most openhearted form welcomes and draws us into the next world in peace.

Loving Guidance

In addition to a loving presence, nearly all the visitors in visitation dreams share a common purpose. The visitor arrives with the express purpose of accompanying the dying person into the next life. In language and gestures the dying person easily understands, the visitors in visitation dreams make it clear they have shown up solely for the benefit of the dying person. They have come to welcome the dying person home, or into the light, into heaven, through the golden door, across the bridge, out the window, onto the train or plane—the images of transition might be anything, but the guides, be they angels or family or Jesus or Buddha, are there to help.

In the 1960s and 1970s, Karlis Osis and Erlendur Haraldsson surveyed doctors and nurses from two vastly different cultures—the United States of America and India—about what they had witnessed of dying people. They found the vast majority of waking, visual "apparitions" of deceased loved ones or religious figures spoke clearly of helping the dying person move to the next life.

> The main ostensible purpose of the apparition is to take the patient away to another mode of existence. This purpose is expressed exclusively by apparitions for the dead and by religious figures. In the pilot study, not a single apparition involving a … living individual was described as coming with the take-away purpose.[36]

---

36. Karlis Osis and Erlendur Haraldsson, *At the Hour of Death: A New Look at Evidence for Life After Death* (USA: Whitecrow, 1997/2012), 61.

Sometimes people negotiate the time of departure. The dreamer sighs and says, "They're telling me it's not time yet. Why can't I go now?" Sometimes the dreamer panics with a quick, "I'm not ready!" A few people in Osis and Haraldsson's study saw the visitation dreams as distressing, as they knew such beings could only mean their death was near. While not all were willing to go with their visitation dream visitors, still all believed such visitors were real and were there to help guide them onward.[37]

The Center for Hospice and Palliative Care study included the account of one woman, Barbara, who dreamed of her deceased father and three brothers about a month before she died. She said they were hugging her and "welcoming [me] to the dead."[38] Another study described how a woman named Ruth found her way forward first blocked and then opened to her by her deceased father.

I saw my parents, holding hands. I wanted so much to join them but my father had constructed some kind of force-field to keep me out. He said very sternly, "Not now, Ruth!" In Ruth's final dream her father had returned. I dreamed that I was wandering around in some or other place—I don't know where it was. My father came and found me and led me away. I don't know where we were going, but I was happy to be going with him.[39]

---

37. Ibid., 91.

38. Kerr, et al., "End-of-Life Dreams and Visions: A Longitudinal Study of Hospice Patients' Experiences," 20.

39. Welman, *Death and Gnosis*, Appendixes A and B.

Visitation Dreams and the Afterlife

Visitation dreams of deceased loved ones speak indirectly of an afterlife. Even if the visitors never acknowledge an afterlife, their very presence speaks to the possibility of life continuing. Their presence is a powerful message that they continue to exist after their physical death. Before any messages are passed, before any conversation begins, their presence speaks of continuity beyond the life of this body because here they are, safe and sound. As L. Stafford Betty, professor at California State University, puts it,

> Usually these spirits bring comfort and a sense of wonder, not only for the dying, but also for the family of the dying. ... They "spiritualize" death. They suggest to all concerned that this world is not the only one, but that a "spiritual" world awaits the deceased.[40]

This glimmering possibility of an afterlife shines brightest when dying people are visited by close family members they hadn't yet heard were dead.

Jay Libby, the hospital chaplain in Boston, confronted a situation like this for the first time just recently. He was called to help a family of adult children make an important decision for their mother, who was dying in the hospital. Their mother had just a few days to live and was slipping in and out of consciousness, unable to communicate with them. Unbeknownst to her, one of her adult children had died the day

---

40. Lewis Stafford Betty, "Are They Hallucinations or Are They Real? The Spirituality of Death Bed and Near-Death Visions," *Omega* 53 (November 2006): 37–38.

before in a terrible car accident. Now the remaining siblings were arguing in the family waiting room about whether to tell their mother. They worried the news might shock her and hasten her death, but they also felt burdened by keeping such important news from her.

In the middle of their conversation one of the brothers turned to Libby and said, "Something strange happened yesterday. Mom sort of woke up, she was lying there, and the next thing I know she was calling out, 'I see my father, I see my mother, and your father's here, and oh! Your sister's here, too.'"

Libby said to them, "That's interesting. All those people have long since passed away, and now she's adding your sister to that list. What do you think that means?" The son answered, "Maybe she already knows our sister is gone; maybe our sister has already come back to be her companion along the way."

The family felt relieved of a tremendous burden. They didn't need to tell their mother about the accident and their sister's death because somehow their mother knew already, and in her visitation dream she saw that her daughter was safe. How she knew was not important for them in that moment, but Libby hasn't forgotten the momentary shiver he felt from this unexpected mystery. He continues to wonder how this woman came to see her daughter at her bedside.

I have heard several stories just like this one told to me from hospice workers around the country. Every now and then a family must endure two tragedies, and surviving family members do struggle to know the right thing to say. Should they tell their dying loved one that someone else they love was just killed? Or should they lie and hope their loved one doesn't think to ask why that person no longer visits? All involved know there is no one right answer to this question.

When the dying person seems to learn this information without anyone having told her or him, families have a choice in how they respond. Some people will see these visitations as proof that life continues and will feel as comforted by the visitation as the person who is dying. Others are left scrambling for an acceptable explanation. They think, perhaps she overheard them from down the hall or up the stairs. Perhaps he merely responded to the tension in the family and made a guess as to its cause.

However it happens, these visitation dreams bring their own peace. Like the mother in Jay's family, the dreamers startle awake and tell gathered family they have just seen a son, daughter, spouse, sibling, or favorite aunt and know it means that person is no longer alive. These visitation dreams don't usually cause new grief to the dying person. The dying person knows their loved one has died, but they also know their loved one still exists and is safe and whole and now present in the room, waiting for them.

Visitation dreams can bring about a transformation in the dying person's emotional well-being, much like the preparation dreams in chapter 2. With their calm appearance, visitors in visitation dreams imply the place where they come from—the place to which they are waiting to accompany the dying person—is peaceful, welcoming, and safe. The emotional intensity of the experience lasts well beyond the impact of regular dreams and can help dreamers move toward death with more hope and acceptance. They offer a glimpse into the mystery of a life beyond this life.

Visitation dreams bring relief to the person who is dying, which in turn relieves the emotional distress of those family members and friends who are with them. There are few things more agonizing than watching a loved one die in fear or distress. When we can't fix them or make them better, when our reassurances have little effect, visitation dreams, by their mere presence, offer us all loving comfort.

Visitation Dreams Assuage Grief

Jay Libby's hospital family found relief in their mother's visitation dream of their sister. Their mother's recognition of their sister told them both mother and daughter would be all right even beyond death. Whenever a dreamer shares a visitation dream like this with family, the dream often becomes part of the family story and is cherished for years. These moments help calm the fears and guilt that come with grief— the worries we didn't do enough, the guilt of living on when someone we love dies, and our yearning to have them whole and at peace once again.

Knowing that the person we love feels safe, held, and hopeful in their last moments brings us peace, no matter what we feel about the afterlife. For those who believe there is nothing after life and that death marks the end of a person's soul as well as body, these visitation dreams can still bring peace and relief. Even if they know a dream can never be a true visitation, if that dream brings comfort to the person who is dying, everyone involved will feel comforted as well. Families feel relief that their loved one's suffering is lessened. It is a profound moment when a living being stops living, and if that final ending moment can happen in peace and tranquility, the family is also relieved of suffering. They can see their loved one is no longer so afraid. A peaceful death is a gift to all who are connected to that person.

For the families who do believe in an afterlife, watching their loved ones reach out in the last weeks of life toward an unseen but welcomed visitor can bring a profound message of hope. Like Kathy with her mother, they find themselves in the presence of a mystery that is greater than their life. The person they love becomes a bridge into a world they can't visit themselves, filled with people they also might long to see. Dreamers are transformed from merely a poor, suffering body into a kind of spiritual pioneer, someone who has seen a distant land and is able to tell about it. The visitation dream can become a gift to everyone who has the privilege of hearing it, from families and friends to caregiving staff. The visitation dreams give all involved something to hope for with their own eventual final moments.

The Meaning of the Afterlife Belongs to the Dreamer

People who face life-ending illness will sometimes begin discussions with their caregivers about the afterlife. They will ask their caregiver what the caregiver thinks about death and spirituality. These questions are not meant to be prying, but to open conversations most find too risky to share with others. It is like testing the waters to see if the other person can talk about such things easily enough.

But how should one respond? Most professional caregivers shy away from answering for fear of closing the conversation before it begins. Fiona Martins, the hospice nurse in Toronto, understands the underlying need to be in a real human conversation, so occasionally she will share her own spiritual beliefs as a way to encourage them to talk to her. Her patients and families are grateful that she helps them explore their beliefs. They don't necessarily want to hear someone else's opinion, but allowing the conversation helps them find their own. They need to find their own meaning for the presence of a deceased relative in their room.

Jay Libby finds that people don't ask him what the visions mean as much as they ask for permission to explore the meaning for themselves, once they have been reassured the experience is real. Libby responds with genuine openness to their experience. "I tell them that it's not unusual for this to happen, but we're not sure what it is. I ask them to tell me more about what their experience has been like for them, which leads to further conversation, begets further sharing."

Libby reassures dreamers that they are allowed to make sense of their experience according to their own beliefs. Like most people who work in end-of-life care, his work is less about finding out whether a visitation dream is objectively real and more about how the dreamer understands the dream. He asks, "What was it like for you?" "What did you feel?" "How do you think about it now?" The dreams help Libby open conversations about what the dreamer thinks about their faith, life, and death.

There is a barrier between our physical life and what—if anything—lies beyond. Some have called it the veil between worlds; others describe a river that, once crossed, cannot be crossed again. Religions have given us Heaven, paradise,

Hell, a return to mother earth, karma and reincarnation, enlightenment, and nothingness.

Ancient Egyptians, well known for their elaborate burial rituals, built the great pyramids as tombs for their rulers. They invented the practice of embalming and mummification, and they carved into tomb walls their fervent prayers and protective spells to help the deceased find their way in the afterlife. These prayers and spells eventually formed the Egyptian Book of the Dead. And still, questions about what comes after life remained. In the tomb of Pharaoh Wahankh Intef, who ruled ancient Egypt around 2000 BCE, a songwriter added a poem in a small space on the tomb walls. He acknowledged all the prayers and imaginings of the next life but he still had his doubts. He wrote,

> None comes from there
> To tell of their state
> To tell of their needs
> To calm our hearts
> Until we go where they have gone.[41]

Four thousand years later, we know no more about the afterlife than these people did. We guess, we believe, we hope (and doubt), but we don't know, not really, not for sure. What comes next remains as much a matter of belief now as it was four thousand years ago, as it has always been.

---

41. Miriam Lichtheim, *Ancient Egyptian Literature: A Book of Readings Volume I: The Old and Middle Kingdoms* (Berkeley: University of California Press, 1975), 196.

We will all face this moment at some point, when we realize we can't know for sure what lies beyond and will have to rely solely on our beliefs about what comes next. I have learned from my work in hospice that we all have questions. People of strong faith and people who are reasonably sure nothing happens next all have moments of wondering again as they approach the end of their lives, and I am sure I will do the same. We just don't know for sure—not like we know the earth; not like we know our own bodies. We have no direct experience of being dead to draw upon, and so we must approach this moment with our trembling ignorance.

If at some point the dying person has a visitation dream of a loved one bringing peace and help to guide them home, there is no reason to chase it away. These dreams are a rare grace note at the end of a long, arduous journey, a moment that can utterly transform a person's death from one of fear and apprehension to one that includes an unexpected joy, peace, wonder, mystery, and grace. Visitation dreams are one way we can step gingerly into the mystery of life and death. By welcoming into our waking lives the presence of our dead, we take one small step beyond what we can know for sure and confront something beyond our comprehension.

When people reach out to unseen visitors with wide smiles and open arms, the dying moment becomes sacred. When they tell these dreams to trusted family members, the dreams become a door into conversations about these mysteries, about what they finally, truly believe. Some family members will find their own spiritual beliefs renewed and others will feel their beliefs challenged. People without any particular belief may find emotional relief and a welcome peace from the visitations, while those with strong beliefs may feel a renewed trust in the possibility of something more, something beyond physical life. As the years pass, families gather and remember the pain of watching someone they love die, but they also remember when joy and a radiant peace broke through the grief and held them in a loving embrace.

Kathy knew she had witnessed something both extraordinary and deeply moving. The moment validated for Kathy the closeness she felt to her mother and helped her let go of the many hurts between them. She felt she had been gifted with the visitation as much as her mother and has held on to it ever since as a sign to her that existence is bigger than humans have imagined and that something—and someone—is waiting for all of us.

Chapter Summary

Visitation dreams are deeply personal and most often bring strong emotions of love and care. The visitors appear objectively real, sometimes bringing the dying person news they could not have known another way. Nearly all visitors in visitation dreams provide reassurance and guidance, accompanying the dying person onward. Those who are fortunate enough to have a visitation dream or witness one often feel their personal beliefs strengthened. Many are moved to accept their visitors with gratitude and a deep sense of peace. Visitation dreams speak so calmly (if indirectly) of an afterlife, they raise new hopes and reassurance about what happens after death.

Talking about Dreams

- What matters most to you about visitation dreams?

- Has someone you loved ever described a visitation dream? How did you respond?

- Who would you want to see at the very end of your life? What would you want them to tell you?

Chapter Five

Dreams of the Community

Death is in many ways a communal event. We are connected to each other through love, responsibility, obligation, and friendship, through the time we spend together and all the ways we hold each other in our hearts and minds when we are apart. Each life is woven tightly into the emotional lives of all those who surround us, binding us to this particular place and these specific people.

Because of these connections, people who are ill are not the only ones to dream at the end of life. At the end of a person's life anyone who is involved with that person, no matter how tenuous or distant the relationship, can be affected by his or her death. Family, caregivers, loved ones, friends, colleagues, distant relatives—anyone who knows and loves the person who is dying—will also dream. Anyone can reach for dreams to help them face the death, adjust to the emotional upheaval, and make sense of their loss. End-of-life dreams for the dying person's community can be comforting or challenging, but ultimately all help the dreamer prepare for grief and loss.

End-of-life dreams in advance of the death don't all look alike, and they don't all touch on the same emotions. They express each dreamer's personal relationship to the dying person and the dreamer's views of death. Some end-of-life dreams are like nightmares with images of destruction and threatening situations. Others present a simple image of such gentleness that the dreamer feels calmed when they awake. There is no universal dream for the people connected to the dying person any more than there is one universal path of loving that person.

Dreams of family and friends of a dying person seem to come with the same purpose as all dreams—to help the dreamer in his or her own life. Some dreams come to give fair warning time is short. In other dreams family members wail the grief they cannot express openly to their loved one. In some dreams, friends and family practice saying goodbye and letting go, over and over again. When people find a way to share these dreams they strengthen their friendships with each other, and this allows them to mourn their loss together.

Give Us Fair Warning

The end of life has as many questions and meandering trajectories as any other time of life, and the physical signs of impending death aren't always clear. Doctors and nurses hesitate before predicting how much longer a person's body will continue. They have all seen unexplained recoveries when moments that look like the final stage suddenly morphed instead into only a mild, temporary setback. They have seen human beings exert an enormous willpower in the last hours of life in order to wait until all their children are present.

Sometimes things do get better. The fever subsides, the cancer stops spreading, the pain lessens, and the breathing deepens and relaxes. What had looked like a final illness instead resolves with antibiotics or a new breathing treatment, and we all sigh in relief. How could we think anything else was wrong?

All of this uncertainty gives us permission to ignore the signs that death is fast approaching. Many people would rather not believe the signs that their loved one is dying, and I include myself in that group. As much as I have sat with people who faced this question, when my own father was nearing the end of his life, I couldn't quite believe it. I pushed my fears aside and hoped along with everyone else that things were getting better and that his condition could improve again.

Our dreams often have other ideas. In our dreams we seem to know better. These dreams can give us fair warning that time is short. They remind us that we are coming to the end of something monumental and we need to take heed of this fact. These dreams can spur people into visiting and calling. Friends dream of saying goodbye to their dear ones and wake up feeling more sure they need to visit. The dreams give them the impetus they need to reconnect and say goodbye before it is too late.

The warnings in dreams give family and friends another chance to embrace the diminishing time they have left. They still face the daunting challenge of talking directly with each other, but with the warning comes the gift of time and a new way into the conversation.

Nicole Gratton and Monique Seguin tell the story of Marielle, a frail ninety-year-old woman who lived in a long-term care facility, and her youngest daughter, Danielle, who at fifty was actively dying of cancer.[42] The other adult children in the family had hesitated in telling Marielle that her youngest was so sick. They didn't want to distress their mother, but they also believed she had a right to know what was happening. When they finally showed up at her room Marielle surprised them all by saying, "You have come to tell me Danielle is not well." She told them she knew because she had dreamed the night before of her youngest daughter climbing stairs and a yellow door. The dream used symbolic language that Marielle immediately understood and held enough urgency for her to act on its message. She insisted her family help her go see her daughter one last time.

Marielle's dream helped her talk to her family about Danielle actively dying and gave them all time to allow Marielle one last moment with her daughter. The family helped her travel to the hospice where Danielle lay in a coma, and Marielle leaned in and softly told Danielle her dream: *"I open a yellow door and I see you. You are climbing stairs. I have spent the night with you, my little one."* According to Gratton and Seguin, a single tear slid down Danielle's cheek, and then the entire family dissolved into tears.

Marielle's dream, with that simple image of opening a yellow door, helped her understand and accept her daughter's approaching death in a way her children's visit might not have done. The dream helped her give an important and beautiful final message to her daughter, and it brought her family closer together. The dream helped Marielle let go of her youngest daughter. It helped the entire family use the

---

42. Gratton and Seguin, *Dreams and Death*, 56–57.

time they had left to say their goodbyes rather than argue over whether or not Marielle should be told.

The hardest grief dreams are the ones that force us to acknowledge our own limits. Sometimes we dream the fantasy so many of us want in waking life of finding the miracle cure and through sheer force of will we get it to our dear one in time. As the end of life approaches, however, our dreams can help us face our inability to cure our loved one. In our dreams the miracle cure comes too late, we get caught in traffic, the elevator stops moving, and we are trapped, helpless, and forced to say goodbye again.

It might be hard to understand why, when we are facing so much loss in waking life, our dreams fill with images of helplessness and more loss. These dreams can help us acknowledge our limits a little bit at a time. It's as if our dreams put us into a desensitization program, exposing us to a harsh reality step by step, allowing us time to get used to what once seemed unimaginable and unendurable. We lose the medicine, then wake up. We fail to save them, then we wake up. We watch them fall, then wake up once again. With each dream we get used to the idea of loss a bit more. We allow this great loss into our hearts one dream at a time.

Give Us Room to Grieve

In their book *Final Gifts: Understanding the Special Awareness, Needs, and Communication of the Dying,* nurses Maggie Callanan and Patricia Kelley tell the story of Becky, a thirty-four-year-old reporter who was dying and didn't want to talk about it.[43] She was not in denial in the classic sense. She had

---

43. Callanan and Kelley, *Final Gifts*, 185–88.

accepted hospice, followed her treatment plan, and kept herself safe. She had accepted she was dying; she just didn't want to talk about it. Becky's husband and the nurse respected her right to not talk and gave her information only as she requested it.

Eventually a dream prompted Becky to talk to the nurse about her questions in one important conversation. The two of them went over what Becky could expect to feel in her body as she died. The conversation comforted her immensely, but my heart went out to her husband, Joel, who quietly left the room to give her the privacy she still wanted. At the end of this conversation, Becky asked the nurse to tell Joel what they discussed, and then she never talked about dying again.

Becky's desire to put off discussing her illness is not uncommon. For some people, talking about what is happening is not an option. Our modern Western culture doesn't give many role models for talking about dying and feelings and grief, leading some people to put off discussing their illness as long as possible, often so they can fully enjoy the life they have left. They simply won't admit to any more illness than they must in order to have as good a life as they can. Like the nurse who eventually helped Becky with her questions, I have respect for those who hate talking about their lives. As much as I want to talk about everything, I know many who feel just the opposite, who might feel burdened by someone else forcing them to talk.

So what is a loving spouse like Joel to do when his wife staunchly refuses to talk about the losses that are piling up all around them? What if Joel is more like me and needs a way to talk about what is happening? How does he keep his own emotional balance while respecting her right to not talk about it?

Callanan and Kelley didn't talk about what Joel felt or wanted, but I am hoping he had some way of exploring his own grief. Who knows—he may have had the same attitude toward dying as Becky—but more often I've seen people like Joel suffer from the lack of communication. Caregivers want to respect the person who is ill, but caregivers are also in grief and some will need to talk about it. They are also losing someone precious, and they will need time to ready themselves, even if the person they love wants to look the other way.

Dreams can give families and friends a chance to express their grief without upsetting the person they care for, who is still very much alive and needing their care. It is a private grief in a private space in which they can acknowledge—at least to themselves—their personal sense of loss. I keep an eye out for the Joels of the world, who keep silent to respect the wishes of others, because I was in that position myself when my father died.

My father was a highly rational man who kept his emotions well hidden. In his last year of life, he wasn't dying from an illness; he had taken a bad fall and was not recovering. Because there was no illness to point to, some in my family held on to a strong, determined hope that he could get better. I could see he had taken on the look of so many of my hospice patients, but I wondered if maybe my work had made me see death everywhere. I debated whether I should hang on to my family's hope and push him to get well. Then he fell again and landed in the intensive care unit. One night soon after that, I had this dream:

> *I watch two middle-aged men cheer on their team at a football game, and I know one of them is my father, young again and full of energy. The two men are stripped to the waist, painted blue, and they jump up and down screaming, arms waving and beer sloshing, willing their team on to victory. And then their team does the unthinkable. They lose. My father falls back and begins weeping—great heaving sobs of anguish. I feel shocked by the rawness of his pain, but I can see he isn't bitter or angry. He is completely involved in this game—crying at the loss is all part of the full experience, the only response to have when so much is at stake. By the end of the dream I am crying with him.*

When I woke up I lingered in bed, pondering the dream and thinking about my father. I remembered only rare instances of him expressing a stronger emotion than a frown or a deep chuckle, yet in my dream he seemed satisfied, even proud of his emotional outpouring. Despite the wailing—or maybe because of the wailing—he was enjoying himself.

I knew my dream was about my grief. Despite the reassuring, hopeful messages I was hearing from family, I had to consider my father might very well be dying. And in my dream, at least, he was ready. I felt reassured that even as he was losing this game and even though I was going to lose him, he was still being held in a kind of joyful reverence for the game he had played well up until then.

This was a dream I needed to have. It gave me permission to pay attention to my grief and to not push it aside as inappropriate. The dream reminded me that I wanted all my feelings, no matter how painful, because that is how I play the game, too.

Dreams at the end of life help everyone involved face the loss and all the emotions that come with losing someone we love. In grief dreams we can yell and scream our frustration, beat our fists against the wall, drive our cars over cliffs in desperation, and still wake up safely. In dreams we can love our dear ones unabashedly and hate them for leaving and beg them to stay. These dreams can be cathartic and enlivening. When we allow our emotions an outlet, even if it is only in dreams, the energy we had been using to hold them in is released.

Anyone in a person's family or community can have a grief dream. Everyone in the entire community has the chance to say goodbye as many times as we need. In these dreams we hold on to the people who are dying, reach out to them, and say goodbye again and again until we lose our breath, until we can breathe in the loss.

Help Us Let Go

Sometimes dreams help families find the strength and peace to let their loved ones go. Nicole Gratton and Monique Seguin tell of a dream similar to mine of a woman named Francine, who was the only child of an eighty-four-year-old woman. Francine's mother had been in good health until she suffered a serious injury from a bus accident. Like me, Francine wanted

only for her mother to recover until she had a dream that told
her something different.

> *I arrive at my mother's apartment in Montreal. She has*
> *painted everything yellow. I want to intervene and tell her*
> *to paint the ceiling white. ... I meet Aunt Suzanne*
> *(deceased for several years) [who tells me,] "Let her be.*
> *After all, she knows that she has little time left." I feel that I*
> *must let go.*[44]

In light of the dream, Francine wondered if she needed to
allow her mother the emotional room she might need to die.
The dream helped Francine question whether she was seeing her mother's desires clearly. It helped her recognize her
own fear of loss buried within all her helpful pushing of her
mother toward recovery.

This story reminds me of so many families searching for
ways to help their loved one recover from serious injuries.
I have met with many families of people in intensive care
units who are searching desperately for a cure or treatment
to bring their loved ones back to their previous level of health
again. I imagine Francine hoped her mother could adjust to
her new life of physical dependence long enough to make a
full recovery, just as my family hoped our father would recover. Most families in this situation want what is best for
their loved ones and most are sure, especially in the early
hours after injury, that what is best must be a full recovery.
Like Francine, most of us will try to will our loved ones to
recover. We bustle into their rooms full of cheer and encour-

---

44. Gratton and Seguin, *Dreams and Death*, 49–50.

age them to eat more and do their exercises. We chat about our day and the future in such a state of hopefulness that it is hard to take into consideration the possibility that our loved one might have other ideas. Sometimes families need a dream that whispers another possibility.

Francine was surprised by her dream aunt telling her to let her mother be, but as Seguin puts it, "She understands that she must not pressure her mother; she must allow her to be free to do anything she wants to." This is a tremendously difficult decision for a loving child to reach, but Francine's dream seemed to be telling her that all her encouragement might not be what her mother wanted. Her dream helped her come to the conclusion that perhaps "it is better for mother to live fully for six months than to barely exist for many years."[45]

Francine's dream helped her step back from her focus on helping her mother improve and remember her mother's lifelong need for autonomy and independence. She allowed the dream to influence her relationship with her mother, and it helped prepare her emotionally to let go. She was ready when four months later her mother's health suddenly took a turn, and she was admitted to the intensive care unit.

I imagine their relationship improved during those four months as well. Even the closest relationships have tension when two people are working at cross-purposes. When Francine stopped pushing for recovery and took more time to enjoy her mother's company, I can believe her mother also relaxed, basking in the newfound appreciation. Their time together

---

45. Ibid., 49.

was colored again by their emotional closeness, rather than conflicting hopes and plans.

And then Francine's dream connected with her mother's life in a way that felt both beautiful and mysterious. On a visit Francine asked her mother if she had slept well the night before and her mother replied, "I must have slept because I had a dream: *I am in a strange place. I see that everything is yellow. I feel fine.*" [46] She died the following day.

With her mother's final dream of a yellow room, Francine felt held in the connection between the two dreams. The color yellow is often associated with light and warmth, such as from the flame of a candle or the rays of the sun. Francine's own dream of a yellow room now felt supportive and reassuring to her, as if she saw—and her mother had glimpsed—the same room, had felt the same warmth.

In many ways, Francine and I were in the same situation. We both wanted to encourage our parent to recover from a serious injury. We each had a dream that prompted us to reconsider what our parents wanted for themselves. Our dreams were radically different from each other: Francine dreamed about an all-yellow room she wanted to paint white, and I dreamed of my father as a middle-aged man sobbing when his football team lost. When we each woke up, however, we both wondered if we should reconsider what our parents wanted for themselves.

Sometimes dreams give us our own private space in which we can say goodbye. If we are not able to be with our loved ones, sometimes a dream provides the protected space we need to say our goodbyes. My friend Kay was away at

---

46. Ibid., 50.

college when her grandfather died. She knew he had moved into a hospice but couldn't get back in time to see him. Then one night she had a dream: *He was packing his suitcase. Nothing more than that, but I woke up feeling ... glad for him. He looked happy.*

Kay was not particularly interested in dreams at the time. She still doesn't remember her dreams very often and up until that dream had never considered one to be predictive. When she awoke from this dream, however, she took a moment to hold her grandfather in her mind. She felt as if her dream gave her the chance to say goodbye to him. What's more, she felt sure he was ready and at peace. In her dream she had seen him packed and ready to depart on an adventure that made him happy, and she felt pleased for him. She wasn't surprised to learn he died a few days later.

Dreams of leave-taking can be this simple and direct. Family and friends dream of letting go, saying goodbye, and watching loved ones leave, and they wake knowing this dream came to help them say goodbye. These dreams often use the same journey images as the preparation dreams of people who are dying, with one important difference. The dreamers see their loved ones traveling, while they remain at home. In the peaceful versions of these dreams, the dreamers watch their loved ones pack, close up shop, buy a ticket, and go stand in line. They watch as their loved one boards a train, sails away, or flies off in a plane, while they themselves remain on the ground and wave goodbye. The dying person is often seen as whole and healthy again, happy and looking forward to the trip.

In many ways, these are grief dreams showing up before the person has died, in anticipation of the loss families must face. They are a natural part of grief as each individual prepares himself or herself for a future without that person.

Connect Us Across Great Distances

As Kay's experience shows, dreams can help connect family members who are not able to gather when someone is dying. Work and family obligations, lack of money for travel, and the uncertainty of knowing when a visit would help the most all make it hard for people to be with their loved ones at the exact moment of death. In my work I have met many loving people who simply could not be at the bedside when they most wanted to, for a host of reasons.

In dreams, however, families can stay as close as they want to be. They can visit their loved ones in dreams, put their arms around each other, and walk together down leaf-strewn country roads. In dreams they can reach out across vast distances that separate them and say the things they most want to say.

I know dreams of being together are not the same as physically being together. They cannot take the place of actually being together, but they are better than no dreams at all.

My friend Kay felt the comfort of this type of dream when her grandfather died. She couldn't be there, but her dream helped her feel close to him. She felt that closeness again years later when her uncle was dying. He was the brother-in-law of her aunt—an uncle by marriage that she didn't see often. He vacationed with her family for several summers when she was little, and she saw him occasionally at family parties. He was a successful artist, and when Kay was in college she often brought her fellow art students to his gallery openings. As Kay moved into her adult life and a creative career of her own, her uncle moved out of the area to follow his art. They stayed in touch only sporadically, but many years later their paths crossed again.

"A book came out that was a retrospective of his work and he sent me a signed copy through my aunt," Kay shared with me. "I was so touched and told my aunt I should thank him—write him a letter or call—and my aunt said, 'Why don't you go see him, he's in the hospice.' That's when I knew he was dying."

Kay looked for a time in the next several days when she could visit him. A few nights before she was to see him, she had a dream of visiting him in his home.

In my dream his place was also full of interesting stuff, like an artisty-type place—not what his apartment really looked like. He was being very eccentric—very much the artist—and there was a student hanging around, like a demonstration of how the world saw him, that a student would be eager to have him as a mentor.

The next morning she woke to the news that he had died. Despite her shock and disappointment of not seeing him, she felt she had seen him, somehow, in her dream. She explains,

I felt that the dream was in lieu of the visit, in some way; since we couldn't actually meet in person, we would meet in the dream. Which implies that I think he knew about it too, which I don't necessarily think, but it felt like that. That maybe he knew that we had had our visit. Afterward I was glad that I had had the dream. It was enough.

Kay's dream helped her feel again the emotional connection she had with her uncle. The dream didn't pay any attention to his current physical state or the hospice in which he lived, or how he might be feeling about her upcoming visit. Instead, in her dream she remembered his life, the qualities she admired, his quirks and habits of personality, his flair, and his reputation as an artist and a mentor. She woke up feeling as if she had revisited the essence of her relationship with him. She dreamed of what she will remember most fondly about him and the lessons she will carry forward in her own work about artistic freedom and integrity.

Kay's dream also gave her peace that somehow she had found a way to reach her uncle before he died. She feels comforted not just by the dream, but also by its timing with the moment of his death. The way in which her dream and his dying came together in his final night made her feel as if in her dream she had been able to see him and say goodbye.

The coinciding of a dream about a loved one with that person's physical death is a profoundly moving experience. The dreams that come so closely bound to the moment of death give dreamers a visceral sense of being connected beyond death to those they love. They give the dreamers a sense of realness and can lift the dream into a spiritual moment. They make the dreamers wonder if they can travel in their dreams and actually, truly embrace the people they are missing. Some will know after such a dream that there truly is something about us that continues after our bodies die.

The dreams of such exquisite timing such as Kay's dream may not be as rare as they appear. I have heard stories like hers from many people who were wakened from a dream of saying goodbye by the phone ringing, bringing news of that person's death. More than other dreams, these raise the question of just how connected we are to the people we love.

Dreams connect us across long distances even without this close timing. We connect with each other emotionally when we dream about each other, just as if we are sending our best wishes. Our dreams focus our best intentions on the other person, and we wake with their well-being in mind. To wake from such a dream feels satisfying, as if we have reached out and embraced them. It is our way of holding the people we love close to our hearts. They are in our prayers, our thoughts, our love, and our dreams.

Help Us Mourn Together

If dreaming at the end of life has had little attention, families who share their dreams with each other—and how that sharing might help with grief—has had no attention from the research whatsoever. Nonetheless, we can find instances of families doing just this kind of dream sharing, and it gives us a glimpse of what possible benefits talking about dreams might bring.

Michele Chaban noticed the families of the children she worked with occasionally shared their dreams with each other in the waiting rooms and hallways. "Family members would begin to ask each other, 'Did you have dreams?' They noticed their dreams and talked about them between and amongst themselves."

All the positive conversation about dreams between Chaban and the children, between Chaban and the families, and between the staff and the children gave the family members encouragement to remember and think about their own dreams. They found a new source of comfort in their dreams and a new avenue of support with the other family members.

Chaban recalls, "It gave them something important to talk about other than the illness." She notes that most families talked of their good dreams and stayed away from the anxiety dreams and nightmares. They used their dreams to express their love and strength, not fears and anxieties. They shared the dreams that would help build hope and healing.

I think of Chaban's story in chapter 2 about the little girl who dreamed of her deceased grandmother welcoming her with open arms. That one powerful image brought everyone a sense of being held. Dreams of a more mundane nature can also be powerful connectors.

Imagine that same little girl's aunt sharing a dream of the little girl swinging on her favorite swing on a beautiful sunshiny day and laughing, just like she did last summer at the family picnic. This image of a simple pleasure from their shared past can bring the entire family a moment of pleasure, and the girl a moment of remembering what it felt like to swing so boldly. The aunt's dream also becomes a gift for the family, helping them reminisce about the picnic and maybe other family get-togethers, maybe how vibrant the little girl has always been. Dreams like these give everyone something concrete to hang on to, to remember, and to encourage and support each other.

When family members share their dreams with each other, they also deepen the emotional bond they feel with each other. Sharing dreams, like all emotional sharing, helps reduce the fears and anxieties that grow so quickly in isolation.

Dream worker and author Robert Moss tells the story of Valerie, a young hospice volunteer who worried about her mother, a woman who was dying and very frightened.[47] Valerie wanted nothing more than to help ease her mother's fears, but her mother was too frightened to talk about dying. One night Valerie had a dream in which she and her mother and all of their relatives, both living and long dead, partied together in a beach house. Valerie woke feeling relaxed and energized, and when her mother called her later that morning, she told her mother about the dream. After a pause her mother said, "The whole family was together last night in my dream, too. I am always in that beach town in my dreams now; that is the only place I go to anymore."

This shared dream became a bridge for Valerie and her mother. Valerie now had one image to help her mother through the dying process. From then on, she encouraged her mother to revisit the beach town whenever her mother felt anxious, and the dream gave them a way to share the hope of meeting departed family and old friends again. Valerie told

---

47. Robert Moss, *The Dreamer's Book of the Dead: A Soul Traveler's Guide to Death, Dying, and the Other Side* (Rochester, VT: Destiny Books, 2005), 254.

Moss, "I found a way to help her move through her fear of dying, without ever even mentioning the word *death*."

I have seen many families drift apart right at the moment when their presence is most important. Many people shy away when they can't find something concrete to contribute. We don't trust that our presence is enough, and we lose out on the comfort that being in this together can bring. In the waiting we all do at the end of life, dreaming and sharing our dreams can become something we offer. Our dreams become more like prayers of benediction and healing. It gives everyone a chance to share something of hope with the larger group. Everyone is participating, involved, and an integral part of this event.

When families share dream images that touch on the end of life, they are acknowledging that the dying is happening to everyone. When families can share their wishes for healing and fears of loss through their dreams, they find another way to acknowledge their feelings. They find company for their journey through grief.

Chapter Summary

Dreams at the end of life are not only for the people who are dying. Anyone connected to the dying person—families, caregivers, friends, and colleagues—can dream about the loss they each must face. Dreams of this wider community help by giving us fair warning that time is running out. Our dreams can help us face the truth in time to be fully present. Dreams give us a safe place in which to begin grieving the death of a loved one who can't or won't talk with us about what is happening. Dreams help us say goodbye by giving us sometimes painful images of letting go, losing our grip, and dropping back and being left behind. Through our dreams we can walk with our loved ones who live far away from us and wake feeling emotionally connected with them. When we tell these dreams to others, we open a new opportunity to talk and mourn together. In this way the dreams can become a gift to an entire community.

Talking about Dreams

- Has a dream ever helped you face a hard truth you had been avoiding? How did it help?
- Has a dream ever helped you feel close to someone who was living far away?
- How has a dream helped you prepare for a loved one's death?

Chapter Six

Grief Dreams Help Us Mourn

Of all the dreams that come around the end of life, grief dreams are talked about most often. Nearly 85 percent of people who responded to one survey said they'd had a dream of a deceased relative.[48] They may be the most common dreams people have around the end of life, although not enough researchers have asked about the other types of dreams to know for sure. Grief dreams bring one last meeting between mourners and their loved ones, one more chance for mourners to hold them, make amends, and reassure themselves their loved ones are safe, whole, and at peace. Even people who don't, as a rule, remember their dreams want at least one grief dream they can hold on to and cherish.

Experts in the field of grief counseling often talk of three different periods, stages, or seasons of grief. When written down, these stages follow a natural progression from the initial shock of loss, through a stormy, chaotic period of disorganization and search for meaning, before the bereaved finally

---

48. Craig M. Klugman, "Dead Men Talking: Evidence of Post-Death Contact and Continuing Bonds," *Omega* 53 (2006): 258.

emerge into a new life that both feels whole and encompasses the loss. In research, this progression is well-defined and orderly, but real life is seldom so tidy.

In life, the human heart seems to swoop through all these stages and back again in less than an hour. While most people feel stunned in the initial shock of loss, for instance, that stunned feeling can dissipate within a few minutes or linger for months or return in force when a new stressor hits years in the future. The timing is always in the hands of the mourner.

Just as grief doesn't always follow a well-timed progression and follows instead the needs of the person in grief, grief dreams also follow the needs of the dreamer. Grief dreams don't all come with the same purpose or show the same images. Instead these dreams follow the life of each mourner and the relationship the mourner has with the deceased. In her book *The Dream Messenger,* dream expert Patricia Garfield considers twenty of the more common messages found in grief dreams and how often they seem to contradict one another.[49] She noted that for every dream that shows our loved ones well and whole again, someone else's dream shows them suffering. For every dream of a loved one reaching out in love, another dream shows them walking away without a backward glance.

The research team at the Center for Hospice and Palliative Care asked family members about their dreams after the death of their loved ones and found the same wide variation. Here are a few of the dreams they gathered:

---

49. Patricia Garfield, *The Dream Messenger: How Dreams of the Departed Bring Healing Gifts* (New York: Simon and Schuster, 1997).

- *I occasionally dream of my sister. She is younger with long hair—not the way she looked at her death.*

- *The times my mother was in my dreams and never spoke made me feel sadder.*

- *My mother speaks to me while I dream. I get to hold [her] in my dreams and get to feel her warmth and love.*[50]

These are all typical grief dreams. They reflect not just the person who died but also the dreamer and the nature of the relationship between the two. Dreamers can wake feeling comforted, challenged, saddened, held, or shocked by the images. For all the different images, themes, and messages of grief dreams, however, the dreams do all serve the same specific purpose. Each dream arrives to help the dreamer mourn. Grief dreams help us through the initial shock and numbness by showing us the person we love saying goodbye and looking happy or by replaying their final moments in frightening images, until we accept that the death happened the way that it happened. Dreams help mourners through the chaotic, disorganized middle stage by reliving and sorting through the conflicting emotions one by one, putting each into a new perspective. They help dreamers in their search for meaning and for one last moment with their loved one. Dreams help mourners create a new relationship with those who died, which helps them rebuild and recenter on their own lives again.

---

50. Scott T. Wright, Christopher W. Kerr, Nicole M. Doroszczuk, Sarah M. Kuszczak, Pei C. Hang, and Debra L. Luczkiewicz, "The Impact of Dreams of the Deceased on Bereavement: A Survey of Hospice Caregivers," *American Journal of Hospice and Palliative Care* 31 (2014): 132–8.

Shock

The first thing most of us feel when someone dies is shock. Our bodies, minds, and hearts go numb as we try to process the information into reality. It just doesn't feel real at first. It takes time to understand fully that someone we love is not coming back. Most of us know this only intellectually at first. We tell ourselves and our friends, of course she died, of course he's not coming back. We talk about the person who died and exactly what happened at the time of death. We understand in our minds what death means. But it takes longer to stop reaching for the phone to call them. It takes longer before we stop catching glimpses of them on the street and whirl around, startled, to make sure. Slowly we stop making room for them in bed or picking up the special foods they loved or rushing home before they worry. They will continue to live in our hearts for the rest of our lives, but it takes time for our bodies—our reflexes, habits, and assumptions—to accept and eventually to expect their physical absence.

Show Us the Reality of the Person's Death

Grief dreams can help us understand the person who died is truly gone. No matter what images grief dreams bring, whether they are comforting, frightening, or bewildering, the images help us acknowledge their death and our loss. They help us accept our loved ones' physical absence.

- *In my dreams I see him lying there in the last few minutes of his life.*

- *She was in a group of three or four people and just smiled at me. She didn't say anything, but she looked healthy and at peace.*[51]

It isn't hard to imagine someone having such dreams in the first weeks following the death. The first example pushes the dreamer to acknowledge the death, and the second example provides some relief that the dreamer's loved one is at peace.

Sometimes these dreams come around again much later in life when we need reminding of our loss. Phyllis Russell is a grief counselor in Toronto who regularly takes referrals from the city's many hospice organizations.[52] She knows grief is not something that needs fixing but is something to be listened to and respected. She helps people face their grief at their own pace, not bothering with an arbitrary timeline for mourning. Russell learned this lesson when she was first starting out in palliative care as a nurse, when she was in her mid-thirties.

Russell's mother had died thirteen years earlier, when Russell was just twenty-two years old. She had dealt with it at the time by refocusing her efforts on building her career and her life. This was a good choice for her, but when she began working in palliative care, a dream helped her approach her own grief once again.

I was sitting in our living room with my mother, and I noticed all these people going to the church. I said to my

---

51. Ibid., 4.

52. Phyllis Russell, bereavement counselor. All quotes from Phyllis are from my interview with her in Toronto, Ontario, in August 2012.

mother, "What's going on at the church tonight?" And she
just gave me a smile. When I kept asking she said, "You
know where they're going." I said no, but she said, "Yes,
you do. Just think. You know where they're going. They're
going to my funeral." And I said, "What do you mean?"
She said, "You know I'm dead. And I can't stay, I have
to go."

Russell is now in her fifties but remembers that dream in vivid detail. In the dream she clearly was not understanding the significance of the funeral procession even with her mother's hints. She didn't remember her mother had died, but her dream mother knew. Russell wasn't ready to hear the answer until finally her mother spelled it out for her: "You know I'm dead. And I can't stay." The dream did more than remind Russell of her mother's death; it opened her to a new understanding of what living on without her mother had been like for her.

Russell had had a good life in the years between her mother's death and this dream. She had lived with her grief and moved on with building her life, as most twenty-year-olds would do. She finished school, found good work, and built a home and family of her own.

Now this one dream gave her another chance to remember her loss. The dream prepared her to help others in her new work as a palliative care nurse. She was better able to meet the grief and loss of others once she had welcomed and appreciated again the grief in her own life. The dream gave her new tools to understand the grief of her clients.

Here is a dream of a man Russell worked with who was grieving the recent death of his wife. In the dream he and his wife renewed their wedding vows in front of friends and family, only to become separated later at the airport.

> *As we go through the airport for our second honeymoon Lisa goes through security first but I get stopped. I can't get through. Lisa says to me, "Don't worry, you'll get here one day."*

This man's dream showed him the insurmountable barrier that now stood between him and his wife, and it helped him again understand the finality of their separation.

The dream gave him a concrete, physical way to understand and express how death had separated him from his wife. His dream of their wedding reminded him their separation was not from a change of heart or a lack of love. It wasn't his fault or hers—he was simply not allowed to follow. His dream helped him acknowledge what this separation felt like for him. It was no longer an ache of emptiness in his heart; now it was a very real, solid security gate he could not pass through no matter how hard he tried. His dream allowed him to push up against the barrier, protest its unfairness, and then look again for her on the other side.

And unlike the barrier he faced in his waking life, this time, in his dream, he could see her and hear from her that she was all right. She could reassure him that she was safe, he needn't follow her, she would wait for him, and one day they would be together again.

Russell explains, "His grief totally shifted when he had that dream. She was telling him that he wasn't ready to come through [the gate] and that she was okay where she was." The dream showed him that he didn't need to give up his feelings for her, but he did need to recognize and respect the barrier now between them.

There was a time when grief counselors urged people to let go of their loved ones and move on with their lives, but today we know our love doesn't move in such a limited fashion. When someone we love dies, they don't disappear emotionally; our feelings for them remain. Even if we can no longer see them we still love them, think about them, wonder about them, listen for their wisdom, and remember our best and worst moments together. Our lives have been changed by their presence, and those changes don't disappear. Our relationship with them continues even as it must change to accommodate their physical absence.

Mourning

When someone dies it can feel like a gaping hole has opened in front of us, as if the world has tilted off its axis and we have to find a new balance without that person beside us. We feel lost and overwhelmed by tasks we used to do without thought. We feel tired, uncoordinated, and clumsy. Grief is not one specific emotion as much as it is a wild ride through too many conflicting emotions to count. Some of us cycle through a dizzying array—fear, rage, yearning, guilt, relief, love, peace, gratitude—before we can make sense of any of them.

This period is the heart of mourning. The emotional disruption can lead us to search for meaning and to reorganize our lives. Mourning always takes as long as it needs to take. Some people find a new balance within weeks, others a few months, and still others struggle in a quiet emotional chaos for years.

Help Us Feel Our Loss

Sometimes grief dreams can help caregivers remember their own importance. I am thinking specifically of caregivers I have met who, without meaning to, lose themselves in the care of another human being. They immerse themselves in the never-ending daily tasks and let go of their own needs. They put off seeing the doctor, stop socializing, and deny themselves even a few hours away. Some stop eating and sleeping for fear even that short time away could cause their loved ones stress. They all but disappear into the demands of keeping their loved one safe and out of pain. They keep their attention on the one who is ill, and they see death as something that is happening only to the one they love and not to them as well. They forget to pay attention to their own perspective and their own loss.

It is a vital step in grief when caregivers and family members can affirm to themselves that they are still alive and that their life still matters. Grief dreams help people find and take that vital first step. Just as a dying person's dream can give the dreamer back a sense of control and dignity, so do the dreams of caregivers remind them that their rightful place is at the center of their own lives.

Grief dreams remind caregivers they are not passive witnesses to someone else's suffering. Their lives are being changed against their will, too. They also suffer. They also feel the small losses pile up day after day. This seems like a simple statement of fact, but it is a fact that too often gets lost in the middle of caring for someone who is ill. Grief dreams bring caregivers back to their own lives; in their dreams their concerns and their loss take priority. Grief dreams remind them they must pay attention to how they will live with that loss. Dreams remind them that what they feel and need is just as important as the needs of their loved ones and that the loss they are suffering matters. Grief dreams remind them that they matter and how they will survive matters.

Grief dreams help by giving us room to explore our strongest emotions. Emotions we might not even have noticed become dramatic landscapes in our dreams, with events and concrete images we can comprehend and push back against. In our dreams we better understand hidden nuances of our relationship, release pent-up emotions, and begin the slow work of making sense out of our loss.

Here are a few images from grief dreams gathered by psychiatrist and dream expert Ernest Hartmann that explore the emotional impact of loss:

- *A huge mountain has split apart and there are pieces lying around. I am supposed to make arrangements to take care of it.*
- *There was an empty house, empty and barren. All the doors and windows were open and the wind was blowing through.*

- *A huge tree has fallen down right in front of our house. We're all stunned.*[53]

The dream images gave these dreamers a new language to describe the depth of their loss. Not just feeling empty, but standing in an empty, barren house with the wind blowing through it. The dreams amplify the emotions to their true dimensions. It is one thing to feel we are responsible for picking up the pieces when something breaks. When the something broken is a huge mountain that has split apart, it describes a force that can rip the very ground out from under us.

None of these three dream examples had images of the person who died or depicted an actual event in the dreamers' lives. Instead, the images displayed a raw emotional power that was immediately clear to the dreamer. The dreams carried a profound sense of loss, and the dreamers knew immediately what these dreams were showing—a seemingly impossible disruption of the earth with everything in pieces, a hollow emptiness, and a home threatened by a dead, fallen tree. What emotions are lying within the wreckage? Feeling lost, overwhelmed, responsible and guilty, empty, barren, stunned, vulnerable, and frightened. Their dreams faithfully reflected the emotional upheaval they experienced in waking life and put them into a physical form that is easier to see and grasp.

In grief dreams we often see our loved one in settings that reflect our own emotions more than they represent the person who died. Tina J. Wray, grief expert and author of *Grief Dreams: How They Help Heal Us After the Death of a Loved*

---

53. Ernest Hartmann, *Dreams and Nightmares: The Origin and Meaning of Dreams* (Massachusetts: Perseus, 1998/2001), 23.

One, gives an example of a man who wants desperately to hear from his brother who died in a kayaking accident.

> *The phone rang in the middle of the night. I knew someone was on the other side, yet I couldn't hear who it was. I guessed it was Charlie but couldn't be sure. I began to feel afraid. I listened intently but realized I was wearing earplugs.*[54]

This dream embodies the mourner's yearning and frustration. The dreamer wants to hear but can't, wants to connect but doesn't know how, is afraid but is still holding on, straining to hear, only to find he had stopped up his own ears. I have heard this frustrated yearning before in other dream settings. The dream images are different but the emotion they reflect is the same: we reach out but can't touch them. We call out but they don't turn around. We feel something—we hope it's them—but can't see what it is. We see their mouths moving, but we can't hear them.

This type of grief dream takes our feeling of loss and projects it out into the image of an immense divide—a chasm that now looms between us and those we have lost. Every time we wake from this type of dream, every time we fail to cross the divide between this life and the next in our dreams, we are reminded again the loss is real, and the loved one is no longer within our easy reach.

---

54. Tina J. Wray with Ann Back Price, *Grief Dreams: How They Help Heal Us After the Death of a Loved One* (San Francisco: Jossey-Bass, 2005), 77–78.

We grieve in dreams like we do in daily life, but in dreams we have fewer restrictions on how we express our pain. In grief dreams we can allow ourselves a full emotional range—rage, howling despair, helpless begging, yearning, tenderness and love, guilt for anything and everything we regret, and searching relentlessly for answers. We put our emotions into dream actions like a kind of dream poetry. Instead of allowing ourselves only a single teary moment, we dream of drowning in an ocean of tears. Instead of asking *Why?* to no one in particular, we scream our whys at the sky, at God, at the person who has died, and sometimes in our dreams they scream back.

The strong emotions we feel when someone dies do not all have to be negative. Sometimes in a dream all our pain can be held and softened by a deeper emotion of comfort and peace. My friend Lee had such a dream about six weeks after a young woman who was driving drunk killed Paula, her partner of twenty years.

In the dream Lee was getting ready to move out of her home. This dream home reminded her of her piano teacher's home; it had a piano, a fireplace, and a beautiful wall of shimmering crystal bricks that gave the darkened room its only light. Suddenly a young woman appeared, grabbed a heavy poker from the fireplace, and began ...

> ... *swinging away, two-handed, at the glass brick wall, smashing it and smashing it and smashing it. Shards and chunks of glass burst into the air of the living room making a radiant, geometric pattern.*

> *Then the moving shards changed pace to a kind of*
> *slow-moving stop-action procession through the air. They*
> *were infused with their own light and glowed and glistened*
> *and sparkled as they flew. My initial horror quickly*
> *changed to awe and wonder. Then I woke up.*

Lee found many insights from this dream, but I want to stay with the emotions this dream showed her. When Lee woke up she could still feel the horror on a visceral, gut level of watching this young woman destroying the crystal wall. She knew what was being destroyed was the life of her spouse, her own life, and their life together. But as strong as that emotion was, it was softened by another, deeper emotion of comfort and peace, a sense of home. The action all took place within a home Lee and Paula had built together with music and warmth and a crystal wall whose light was undiminished by the violence. All through her dream that feeling of comfort and home-ness remained, even when the glass was being smashed. The light wasn't destroyed at all; Lee could see each shard of glass was infused with the same sparkling, glowing light.

The dream helped Lee know this one incident of horror couldn't end their love or who they were together, or who they continue to be together. The accident wouldn't negate what they had built. Lee's dream showed her how to hold on to the greater goodness of her relationship with Paula and the home they had created together.

These grief dreams feel like us—our dreams about our grief, our own hearts, our lives and our insights. And from this perspective, dreams give us enormous help. As one part of us, they help us make sense of our loss and our relationship. They help us find healing in the midst of our hardest days. In these dreams we can better understand our own feelings of joy, hope, fear, despair, anger, and ambivalence—all now reflected back to us with the purpose of helping us live through our loss.

Connect Us Again with Those We've Lost

Some grief dreams are so vivid, so real that we wake up sure we have seen our loved one again, as if the person we most want to see has come back from the other side of life across this bridge of our dreams. In our dreams we find them again, often whole and healthy, miraculously unscathed, and bringing messages of love, comfort, reassurance, advice, and peace. We touch their faces, hold their hands, and feel their warmth.

My friend Gail had such a dream. Gail has always been interested in dreaming and has had several important dreams in her life. Two weeks after a close, lifelong friend died of cancer, Gail had a dream that transcended her usual dreams. In her dream, she sat next to her friend, Diana.

> [Diana] is vividly real and looks healthy, although she is thinner than she was in real life. Her pale skin is so clear, almost luminous, her eyes bright. ... Diana is describing meals she and her husband have had ... but I begin to feel uneasy as I remember she is dead. "How can we be sitting here talking when you died?" I blurt out. She doesn't really react—maybe a tiny shrug—and then says, calmly, "I want to know how I was memorialized." I tell her about the service, then reach out to hug her. I'm afraid she will

evaporate, but she is solid flesh and she hugs me back. I
fade into wakefulness.

Grief dreams can feel more like an actual visit from those
we've lost than an act of our imagination. Gail doesn't look
at this dream as her imagination alone. She feels it was a visitation dream—that her friend Diana found a way to visit
her through the dream landscape and say goodbye in a way
that befitted their friendship of more than thirty years. The
dream gave Gail a chance to see and hug her friend goodbye.
It gave her the chance to tell her friend about the memorial
and about how she and all their friends would remember her.
It gave her the chance to say again, "I know you died." Because of its vividness, because it felt like a visitation, Gail felt
her grief lift after their last embrace.

Visitation dreams like Gail's dream invite mourners again
to the great questions in life. Do we continue to exist and
love after our physical death? Is there something beyond life
waiting for us? The dreams blur the line between what comes
solely from our imaginations and what comes as a bridge
between this life and the next. They are powerful messages
of life and love continuing beyond death, and to speak about
them in any other way feels disrespectful to the person who
died and to our own experience. They give us the chance to
say what we might not have been able to before, including
the simple, direct messages of goodbye, I love you, and I will
remember you. They reassure us that we can remain close
despite the separation.

Grief counselor Phyllis Russell has seen many clients wait
impatiently for a dream visit. Most of her clients will seek

these dreams out and worry if they have not yet had a visit from their deceased loved ones. These are not people who consider themselves strong dreamers, and often they don't see the dream they want as in their control. Instead they ask her why their loved one hasn't visited them. Russell says, "They don't expect themselves to dream. They expect their loved ones to visit, as they have visited other people in the family. They'll say, 'My mother dreamt about him, my friends dreamt, my sister dreamt, but he didn't come to me. Why didn't he come to me?'"

Russell understands that what her clients want most of all is to feel they are still connected to their loved one. Or rather, they want to know their loved one is safe and whole, and still connected to them. The sheer force of this desire for connection is breathtaking.

Russell says, "These dreams mean I still have an important part in their life." According to Russell, such a dream is "a validation for their relationship; validation that I am very important in their life, that I'm okay, that I did a good job helping them." In other words, we want to know they will remain close to us, that they choose to remain in relationship with us.

For Russell, these grief dreams tell her more about the dreamer than the dream. She treats each dream the same, asking people to tell her how they felt in the dream and what they think of it now. She helps her clients explore how the dream helps them hold their grief and their (sometimes complicated) love for the person who died. She doesn't take away the possibility their loved one has managed to contact them through the dream, but she doesn't hold that belief herself.

When she talked about her dream of her own deceased mother—described at the beginning of this chapter, when she couldn't figure out who the funeral procession was for—she described it as her dream about her mother, not as her mother's visit to her in a dream. When she woke up, she didn't wonder if her mother had actually been there. She hadn't been experiencing a need to reconnect with her mother. She had needed to reconnect to her own loss and emotional resilience. She saw the dream as about her own grief.

Susan McCoy is a retired police officer and traumatic grief counselor in Toronto who now specializes in counseling families whose loved ones were killed in accidents or during a crime.[55] Like Russell, she also hears clients become frustrated if they haven't yet had a reassuring dream of the person who died. Unlike Russell, however, McCoy does believe some grief dreams bring true connections with people who have died. She has come to appreciate the healing power these visitation dreams bring. For the families of trauma victims especially, I can imagine a dream of a peaceful visit could bring enormous relief and reassurance. The dream becomes another reassurance that their loved one is now at peace and well away from the terrible events that took their life. They can see with their own dream eyes that their loved one is safe and whole and smiling on them.

Occasionally McCoy's clients will fight with themselves, saying, "I'd like to dream of that person but I'm fearful of having a dream, because what's that going to be like?" The

---

55. Susan McCoy, grief counselor in private practice. All quotes from Susan are from my interview with her in September 2012.

dreams might show their loved one is okay, or the dream might show their loved reliving the last minutes of their life, which is a terrifying thought to the families of crime victims.

Because McCoy knows how important these dreams can be, she will help people move past their fears and support their search for a grief dream. One of her clients, the mother of a young son who drowned, was especially conflicted. She wanted to see her son again but was really fearful about it at the same time. As McCoy describes, "She wondered why she wasn't having dreams of her son, but then she would say, 'I can't handle it.'" Helping her client have a good dream about her son became the focus of their work for a time. "We worked together to change her fears. She came to see he wouldn't harm her in any way and that he wouldn't be disturbed by coming to her in a dream." McCoy encouraged the mother to look for the dreams she needed until finally her client was able to have a dream in which she had contact with him. She and her son had the conversation she most needed to have, and she felt grateful.

Susan's clients also contend with friends and family who want them to get over their grief or grieve in a particular way, as nearly all bereaved people hear at some point. Her clients go through an additional trauma, however, of knowing their loved ones died from a violent act. They often live with the agony of not knowing what exactly happened and endure a long, slow legal process to bring killers to justice, complete with intrusive media coverage and whispers about their loved one's character. (Why was she there? How did he know those people?) It is no wonder some clients will come to her in tears after a well-meaning friend or religious leader told them they should stop dreaming of the person they lost and let that person go already, as if they have clung too long to an illusion of connection.

McCoy knows the importance of people fully realizing their loved one is dead and that they physically will never again walk through the door. But she also knows it is just as important that they understand our relationship with them will continue, even as it changes. We will never again have them physically here, but we can find a new way to connect with them, including our trust in their appearance in our dreams.

Grief experts agree that grief dreams of deceased loved ones visiting do no harm to the dreamer, nor do they lead the dreamer away from a full life. In fact, researchers have found just the opposite to be true. People who believe their loved ones have returned in a dream to say goodbye have an easier time accepting their death than those who have had no such dream.[56]

Occasionally McCoy's clients dream about their loved one giving them details of the crime that led to their death, specific details that the police don't know. They wake up wondering if they have just been given a valuable clue from the afterlife, and they ask McCoy if they should tell the police. She supports their decision either way. By supporting their impulse, she helps them trust their ability to judge their own life experience. She keeps herself in the role of a support to them in their grief process, rather than adding to the pressures already on them to grieve in a particular way.

---

56. Nigel P. Field, "Continuing Bonds in Adaptation to Bereavement: An Introduction," *Death Studies*, 30 (2006): 709–714. doi:10.1080/07481180600848090.

McCoy knows the power that can come from trusting their experience enough to act on it. Relaying the information found in a dream can be a healing action. When dreamers act on what they know, even if the information turns out to be wrong, the dreamers know they are respecting the truth of their own experience, which is a powerful feeling in the midst of their uncertainty and helplessness. When they act on the information, they affirm the life of the person they love and the strength of their relationship with that person. They are taking an active role in helping solve their loved one's death and finding a small measure of peace for themselves. They are doing something to help rather than suffering passively.

If people in grief can't find the dreams they want, or their dreams don't bring them longed-for visits from their deceased loved ones, a surprising number will search out mediums for help. Both Russell and McCoy have seen many clients ask mediums to contact their dead loved ones for them. As Russell explains, "That need to connect with a loved one is so great that they will use mediums, even if they have never gone to one before."

Mediums offer to bring them concrete, specific messages that their clients can understand more easily than an abstract feeling of a loved one's presence. They offer a means of communication and, more importantly, they validate what their clients already hope is true, that they are still loved and cherished, that love will overcome death. For many people, these messages are enough to give them the peace and acceptance they couldn't find elsewhere.

The belief that our loved ones will actually visit us in our dreams, as opposed to us dreaming about them, has grown more popular in recent decades. Or perhaps the belief has always been a part of life but now more people feel safe in openly admitting their belief that their loved ones are visiting through dreams. The research survey of mourners from earlier in the chapter noted many people had only one or two dreams of their loved one in the first few years following their death, but these dreams are often powerful and deeply memorable.

Grief dreams—whether they are grief dreams about the person or carry the power of visitation dreams—are often described by dreamers and grief counselors alike as helping lift the burden of grief. They often bring a sense of peace and relief as dreamers wake with a new understanding that their loved one still exists, is safe, and remains emotionally, and perhaps spiritually, connected with them. People who have such a grief dream will talk about a stronger belief in life after death and a new easiness about meeting their own eventual death.

Help Us Build Community

Several months after my mother died in 1997, I dreamed I visited her in her new home.

> *She is living in a small trailer in the Arizona desert where she is working at her pottery and exuding a bubbly gleefulness I have always loved. She welcomes me with open arms. I tell her I've been learning Irish songs in her honor, but she isn't interested. "I'm really focused on my Spanish heritage*

now," she says, turning back to her pots, which makes me
laugh. Always the timing between us was off. Then I
wake up.

I love this dream. It pulls together many different strands of
our mother-daughter relationship, both the good and the
frustrating. Her open-arm welcome, her creative energy, and
her casual inattention to me all felt familiar, both comforting and irritating. Her sharp edge helped me recognize my
mother in my dream. If she had appeared to me with only
sweet reassurances of her undivided attention, I wouldn't
have believed it was her.

A few weeks later I told my father about my dream and
his face lit up. He chuckled at her response to my singing
Irish songs. "That sounds like her," he said, still smiling as his
eyes got teary. For a moment he and I became dream archae-
ologists together, searching through the dream for all the little gestures and words that sounded like her, that felt like her,
because we both wanted so much for it to have been her.

In modern Western culture we have a hard time trusting
our own dreams to help us, let alone the dreams of others.
Sharing my dream with my father, who hadn't remembered
a dream of his own for decades and thought about them even
less often, took a fair amount of trust. I was aware he might
not see anything of worth to him, and I was relieved when he
accepted the dream and leaned in to feel its grace with me.

There is a power in coming together to share our dreams
about our dead. In a few short, bold strokes, dreams capture who this person was and what matters most to us. My
dream helped my father talk about what he missed about my

mother, something he didn't do very often. Sharing dreams helps us to build ties with the people who remain and to share what we remember, what we hope for, what we imagine is happening, and what we wish could be happening for the person we love.

Professor Charles Laughlin has found that the act of dream sharing is common outside Western culture. "For most peoples on the planet, dreaming is a thoroughly social process, and dream sharing is a social act. ... For many peoples, dreams are a matter of social concern. Interpretation of such dreams is often a group activity." [57]

In the more dream-accepting cultures, everyone knows a dream can help more people than simply the dreamer. A single dream can benefit an entire community. People learn in childhood to pay attention to their dreams and share them with their families. This daily practice helps some grow up with enough skill to set intentions to dream for the benefit of others. They learn to trust anyone's dream can offer help with their lives.

My father died many years later, and soon after I had a dream of him that also perfectly fit my relationship with him. It showed him enjoying an afterlife, if somewhat sheepishly and a little awkwardly because he hadn't really expected an afterlife when he was alive. Now in my dream he looked young again, more than a little relieved, and he smiled at me with an unguarded, joyous affection. I woke up feeling relieved to see him so happy. I felt sure he was still himself somewhere, smiling at me.

---

57. Laughlin, *Communing with the Gods*, 265.

I told this dream to my sister Mary, but my dream version of our father didn't match her memory of him at all, and she looked crestfallen. She'd had a different relationship with our father, so much so that she didn't recognize any of his mannerisms. She didn't recognize *her* father in my dream and therefore couldn't find any reassurance. She responded as so many people do, by telling me my dream wasn't really him at all; it was just me wanting it to be him.

Mary needed her own dream, with images familiar to her that honored her particular relationship with her father, before she could feel relief that he was all right. Fortunately, she had such a dream a few months later. He looked and sounded like she thought he would, and he said what she expected and needed him to say. This dream conveyed to her his comfort and reassurance and love.

For those who don't believe in an afterlife, these grief dreams still bring enormous relief. For these people, such dreams are less like visitations and more like an expression of their relationship with their loved one. To dream of the deceased is not very different from actively imagining a needed conversation with them. Mental health clinicians help their clients imagine conversations with someone important who has died to help resolve long-standing conflicts between them. The client's imagination provides both ends of the conversation in these instances, and, done well, clients can find new insights about their relationships. These imagined conversations do not carry the same conviction of a live, in-person meeting, but they are still powerful enough to transform relationships and lives.

Just as in these imaginary conversations, the specific images of grief dreams also depend on our dreaming minds to provide both ends of our conversations. Grief dreams give us the reassurance we crave by showing us familiar images and mannerisms. My sister and I both had dreams that each fit our expectations for our father and our personal relationships with him. In many ways, both of our dreams were more about us than about him.

Beyond our own imagined images, however, grief dreams can carry an added emotional vibrancy that transforms them from a dream *about* the person who died into a dream *with* the person who died, as if the person has returned with a final message. My sister and I shared a deep sense that something in our dreams was more than just our projections; it was a genuine meeting. We both woke knowing our father had visited us. As with the visitation dreams of chapter 4, these vivid grief dreams hint to us that another possibility exists, beyond the confines of daily life. For some, this possibility is based on the spiritual or religious beliefs they've always had. For others, the sense of something more comes directly from the emotional strength of the dream. Mourners can feel the relationship is real and ongoing, even if the dream images are their own, and many believe the person they love has truly returned to them.

I sometimes wonder what it would be like if all my brothers and sisters pooled each of our grief dreams about our parents. How many different versions of our parents would we find? How many different facets of their lives would be revealed if we could find a safe way to express all of our different relationships? Would I even recognize my father in their dream landscapes? It could be that their relationships with our father are so different from mine that their dreams would be meaningless to me. Does that make their dreams or mine less real? How much better would we understand each other by listening to the questions and reassurances of our dreams?

For dreams to be shared, they need to be valued by the group as a whole, however, and that's something that doesn't occur often within families in our modern Western culture. Dream groups and spiritual groups could certainly share grief dreams, but they won't have the added connection of shared childhood memories. When we can share grief dreams like we can share memories with people who knew us way back when, our dreams can help us hold each other through our grief.

Integration

At some point, after weeks or months or years, we find a new balance for our lives. The world regains its familiar patterns and the gaping hole of our loved one's physical absence is slowly encircled by time and memory as we live on into the future without them. We can still feel the hole—we will always remember them and miss them—but slowly our loss becomes one part of a life that has continued; a wound that no longer threatens us but has become part of our living.

In this last period, we find a way to live fully beyond the moment of their death. We find a new rhythm to our days and a new way to relate to the person who died. The person who died is still a part of us but now they reside in a different place in our hearts, with a different role and different rules for how we engage with them. They become our deceased loved ones.

Center Us in Our Own Lives

As we slowly adjust to a life without the physical presence of the people we love, our grief dreams adjust along with us. The center of gravity for our dreams shifts, from managing our grief to once again managing our daily lives. Our dreams become less concerned with whether or not our deceased are safe and happy and more concerned with the problems facing us in our waking lives.

Rather than dreams of searching for the person who died, we wake remembering dreams of new problems we face and challenges we need to meet. Our own lives begin to take precedence in our dreams again. In these dreams we might see our love ones, but they have become more a support or advisor rather than the focus of our attention. We dream again of work, children, friends, old problems, and new worries.

Dave, a man whose father had died in a fire several years back, came to Susan McCoy for help. He told her that he was getting on with his life, but he needed to somehow resolve an intense argument he had been having with his father right before his father died. Now he couldn't stop wishing he'd had more time to talk with his father. He wanted desperately to explain himself better, ask for forgiveness, and settle the guilt he still carried with him.

He explained to her, "If I could put this piece at rest I would be good. I just want to say a few more words, let him know what I meant. I always thought I would have more time."

Susan helped him talk through the argument with her, then encouraged him to ask for a dream about his father, and see what happened next.

Within a few weeks Dave had a dream about his father. In the dream his father didn't say a word but listened intently as Dave said everything he wanted to say. When Dave was finished speaking, his father reached out and gave him a big bear hug.

With that hug Dave woke up and felt everything, finally, was going to be okay. He felt an old heaviness gently lift off his shoulders, like he had no regrets pulling at him. He told Susan, "I was completely forgiven. There are no hard feelings between us anymore, and I feel I can move on."

Dave didn't think his father had come back in a visitation dream to listen to his apology. This wasn't a grief dream, either. Dave was no longer concerned about whether his father was safe and whole in a new life, or whether his father remained emotionally connected to the family. Dave wasn't trying to manage his grief as much as he needed a dream about his father to help resolve an old hurt for his own present life.

This type of healing dream is no longer specifically about the person who died. Now the dream is about us—our lives and our problems. Our loved ones become part of our dream world, and their voice becomes one among many to help us figure out our options or resolve old hurts.

I saw this in my own life. I had a health scare several years after my mother died, and one night I dreamed she showed up at the hospital in full protective mode. In my dream, she strode down the hallways waving her arms and shouting at me, the nurses, anyone who would listen to check the kidneys! Check the kidneys! I woke up feeling like I had support. My dream didn't feel like my mother was actually visiting me even though I recognized her typical high energy. I knew my kidneys were fine (they really were), despite her yelling. But I felt held by the memory of her love and her passionate advocacy for me. The dream helped me reengage with my doctor to solve my problem.

As McCoy explains, with integration dreams "it really is about me living on and getting on with my life. In my dreams, I still need their help and their presence, but they come now in service to what is happening in my life."

Chapter Summary

A grief dream is any dream that helps the dreamer mourn a loss. The dreams in which a deceased loved one appears are the most easily recognizable grief dreams, but any image that allows the dreamer to feel their loss can rightly be called a grief dream.

Grief dreams help us remember to pay attention to our own grief as separate from the person who died. They often serve as an emotional and spiritual connection with the person who died; we dream of them reaching out or walking away, holding us or letting us go. Sharing grief dreams can help families and mourners feel connected with each other as we mourn our loss.

Grief dreams can feel ordinary or extraordinary. They can be comforting or haunting, overpowering or so small we hardly know what to think about them. They can transform our grief and our relationships or confirm the path we have already chosen. Not all grief dreams bring us back into direct communication with the person who died, as we saw earlier in this chapter. And not all dreams of our loved ones feel reassuring, as we shall see in the next chapter on nightmares.

Talking about Dreams

- Have you ever had a dream about someone you loved who died? How did the dream affect your relationship with that person?

- Think about the people closest to you now. Have they had grief dreams? What would be their reaction if you told them about your grief dream?

- How have your dreams of your own deceased loved ones changed over the years?

Chapter Seven

When Dreams Frighten Us

On its surface the dream sounded pleasant and even fun to the researcher.

The dreamer watched her daughter mingle at a party in the home of her daughter's in-laws. There was laughter and drinking and a general overall sense that people were having a good time.[58]

The dream shouldn't have been so disturbing, but the dreamer woke up feeling angry, jealous, and then awash in guilt. She woke up knowing she had not been present in that dream because that party was in the future, a future where she was already dead, and there was her family enjoying life without her. She had wanted to live long enough to see her daughter grow up and succeed in her life, but now she knew she wasn't to have that chance. Now her family would live on, and she would miss everything. A few nights later she dreamed again,

---

58. Scott Wright, researcher with the Center for Hospice & Palliative Care, Toronto, Ontario, personal e-mail communication in January 2014.

this time of her four-year-old grandson telling some stranger in the future, "I don't remember Grandma."

This woman felt angry at dying and jealous of her family for living on while she had to die. Her anger and jealousy brought her guilt as well. As she told the researcher, "I felt guilty when I woke up jealous. I don't like jealousy. So that's why it's a nightmare. I can't be jealous that I can't be there [with my daughter]." [59]

Her jealousy and anger stood directly against her beliefs in what a loving and faithful mother ought to feel toward her family. She loved her children and wanted them to be happy, but these intense feelings of jealousy and anger made her doubt her entire life. The researcher who helped her with these dreams explained it this way: "She often repeated the slogan, 'fear is the opposite of faith,' and stated that she therefore chose not to be afraid. However, her dreams made it clear that she had not eradicated these feelings ... as each dream she reported evoked these very feelings." [60]

Nightmares through Life

Dream experts define nightmares most often by their impact on the dreamers. A nightmare is a dream so disturbing the dreamer is jolted awake, sweating and shaking. This definition often gets stretched in popular culture to include any intense and frightening dream, even if the dreamer isn't

---

59. Scott T. Wright, Pei C. Grant, Rachel M. Depner, James P. Donnelly, and Christopher W. Kerr, "Meaning-Centered Dream Work with Hospice Patients: A Mixed Methods Study," 27. [unpublished manuscript]

60. Scott Wright, researcher with the Center for Hospice & Palliative Care, Toronto, Ontario, personal e-mail communication in January 2014.

awakened by it.[61] Any dream that leaves people feeling lost, anxious, terrified, or sad when they wake, making them dread going back to sleep, could be called a nightmare.

If dreams most often reflect emotions about daily life, then nightmares and their cousins, bad dreams, often reflect emotional distress. Nightmares are common in the population at large—nearly everyone can recount at least one nightmare. At the same time, nightmares are fairly rare in each person's life. According to the International Association for the Study of Dreams website, somewhere between 80 and 90 percent of us have had an occasional nightmare, but only 5 to 10 percent report having a nightmare as often as once a month.[62] Most of us have only a few nightmares in any given year, despite all the stressors we encounter in daily life.

Nightmares show up more often when people face a major life event such as a divorce or a career change. People will have more disturbing dreams in the weeks and months after surviving major catastrophes, such as war, personal violence, or natural disasters. Nightmares can become more chronic when life is under chronic and extreme stressors, such as extreme poverty, dangerous living situations, or chronic, debilitating illness. In the most extreme cases, nightmares can become intrusive and act like post-traumatic flashbacks.

The two most common nightmares are of being chased and falling. Nightmares often begin in early childhood when

---

61. Michael Shredl, "Nightmares and Coping Strategies," presented at the International Association for the Study of Dreams Annual Conference, Virginia Beach, June 2013.

62. "Common questions about nightmares," International Association for the Study of Dreams, accessed September 12, 2013, http://www .asdreams.org/nightma.htm.

we are first chased by monsters. As we get older the monsters may go away or turn into enemy soldiers, gangsters, or wild animals—all chasing us and intent on our destruction. If we are not being chased, we dream of falling from some great height, only to jerk ourselves awake before we hit the ground. Bad dreams may be less visceral, but they still leave us feeling wrung out when we wake up. I have yet to meet someone who truly enjoys feeling frightened and out of control in his or her dreams. Horror movies are one thing—I pay the ticket, I walk in, and I can walk out. I know the horror stays on the screen. But nightmares often feel too much outside of my conscious control for me to truly enjoy being scared by them.

If nightmares and bad dreams come too often, dreamers will wonder what it is about themselves that brings on such terrible images. If they believe dreams come solely from their own brain, they may wonder what hidden emotions need such gut-wrenching events to express themselves. If they believe dreams come from a transcendent reality somewhere beyond them, they may wonder why they are being haunted by such terrible images. Frequent nightmares can lead to sleeplessness, too many awakenings, sleep deprivation, and possibly depression. It is no wonder we turn our backs on nightmares then, as if we can protect our daily lives from their misery by keeping them locked inside their dream state. Most of us wake up and breathe in relief that it was just a dream after all and then shove it back under our pillow. We work hard to forget them and move on.

Michael Shredl, a dream researcher who works in the sleep laboratory of the Central Institute of Mental Health in

Mannheim, Germany, says most people in Western culture respond to nightmares in just this way. "We dismiss them altogether by telling ourselves, 'It was only a dream, it wasn't real, I don't have to think about it.'" [63] But he knows from his research that ignoring a nightmare—or rather, trying to ignore a nightmare—actually strengthens the anxiety we feel about the nightmare, which makes it more likely the nightmare will happen again.

Shredl is not saying nightmares push back with more urgency when we ignore them, as if the dreams themselves are in control of what we remember when we wake up. Rather he is noticing how pushing nightmares away has a paradoxical effect on our dream life. When we push a dream away in fear, we are saying, in effect, that we don't think we can handle the power of the dream. If the nightmare feels beyond our control to manage it, then many dreamers begin to fear having another one. Sleep looks less safe and becomes harder to find. All this added anxiety and sleep disruption makes future nightmares more likely.

What Helps Nightmares

If I can't make a bad dream go away by ignoring it, what can I do? The other choice is scarier but ultimately more rewarding. I can face the dream and respond to it, either by talking back to it when I wake the next morning or by turning around and confronting it while still in the dream.

---

63. Shredl, "Nightmares and Coping Strategies" presentation, International Association for the Study of Dreams Annual Conference, Virginia Beach, Virginia, June 2013.

Like many people, I had a recurring bad dream of being chased when I was young. In my dreams the mythical Bigfoot monster of the Northwest chased me. It never caught me, but I often woke in a panic and had trouble falling back to sleep. I was twenty years old before a friend asked me why the monster was chasing me. I had never thought to wonder. "Well," she said, "why don't you stop and ask it next time?" The idea seemed ludicrous—didn't she know how terrifying this monster was? But she was adamant. "It's your dream. You can ask it anything you want."

A few weeks later I found myself in the nightmare again, running for my life, when I remembered my friend's suggestion. I stopped and whirled around, put my hands on my hips and screamed at it, "Why are you chasing me?!" The monster stopped in his tracks with a confused expression. "Umm, you asked me to chase you, didn't you?"

When I could breathe again, the monster explained he was there to guard a treasure for me, by chasing away anyone who wandered too close. Then he walked with me back through the woods so I could see the treasure for myself. I woke up feeling both rich and protected rather than threatened. That was the last time I dreamed of being chased.

The dream of being chased by something threatening is a common and fairly tame nightmare. The notion that I could turn and face my monster within the dream, however, was a new idea for me. I learned that I had a say in my dreams. I wasn't at their mercy even if I couldn't produce a sweet dream on demand, and this insight gave me confidence to face my fears in future bad dreams. I had learned for myself what researchers like Michael Shredl are now confirming.

Sometimes bad dreams are less about haunting us with an unsolvable agony than about showing us something we need to see, like hidden treasures in my case or solutions to problems we haven't yet admitted were problems. Sometimes nightmares challenge us to look at what is most painful. Over time a nightmare can become less like a monster and more like a good friend who has listened carefully to all our secrets and is now willing to shake us up to help us see ourselves.

The importance of looking closely at what scares us may seem paradoxical. Most of us would much rather close our eyes and run away from danger. It seems backward to move toward what frightens us, but that is exactly how many bad dreams can be resolved. When you respond to a dream, you are taking hold of it and drawing it into a conversation. When you say the dream out loud, write it down, draw it, or tell it to someone, it becomes your dream—you possess the dream instead of the dream possessing you. You climb back into the driver's seat and reclaim your rightful spot as the dreamer.

Talking about the dreams that frighten us puts the emphasis on our feelings instead of on the images. We realize the images of monsters, no matter how compelling, are not the main point of the dream. The main point is how we feel in the dream, and how we feel as we recount the dream to someone we trust. By paying attention to the dream, we bring the power of our waking self, with all our coping skills and logic and rationality, to bear on the dream. We listen and accept there is something to learn.

Nightmares at the End of Life

Throughout this book I have given examples of dreams that challenged more than comforted the dreamer. Life review dreams sometimes replay the most traumatic events the dreamers have endured. Preparation dreams can remind dreamers of what is still left undone, and some can bring terrifying images of physical decay and destruction. Visitation dreams sometimes cause people to shrink back from the welcoming friend or family member, crying out instead, "I will not go with you!" [64] Grief dreams can show distorted images of loved ones suffering or images of our loved ones carrying on just fine without us.

In nightmares at the end of life dreamers find themselves stuck, broken, lost, and occasionally dismembered in a truly gruesome fashion. Some dreamers find themselves in mortal peril as planes crash and ships sink and parachutes fail to open. A young woman who had just been transferred into hospice care dreamed of watching her doctors walk away from her while shaking their heads and declaring there was no hope for her.[65]

Fortunately, most end-of-life nightmares transform over time from frightening and threatening to dreams of peace and benediction. The young woman who dreamed of being abandoned by her doctors kept dreaming throughout her time with hospice, and her dreams became progressively more comforting to her. In her very last dream she found new hope for life beyond her life.

---

64. Osis and Haraldsson, *At the Hour of Death*, 46.

65. Welman, *Death and Gnosis*, Appendix B.

I dreamed about four angels, who were singing a hymn. ...
They told me that they had come to take me, and that my
suffering was nearly over. They were the most beautiful
things I have ever seen.[66]

In a very brief period of time between the end of this woman's treatment and her death, her dreams transformed from their first message that she could no longer expect a cure to a final image of angels ready to take her somewhere new and beautiful. She had hope for an end to her suffering and the assurance that she would journey into beauty.

Several researchers have noticed this same transformation from nightmare to healing dream at the end of life.[67] In chapter 4, psychoanalyst Marie-Louise von Franz spoke about two equally strong messages of dreams at the end of life—the inevitability of the body dying and the dreaming soul's assumption that it will continue on beyond physical death. She found this second message of the soul's continuance becomes stronger and more consistent as people approached the moment of death.

How Nightmares Help

As frightening as nightmares can be, they do have something to teach us. Just as dreams at the end of life can help people find hope and comfort, so nightmares can help people understand and manage the tougher emotions at the end of life. Most experts agree that nightmares carry messages that have

---

66. Ibid.
67. Welman, *Death and Gnosis*; Wright, et al., "Meaning-Centered Dream Work with Hospice Patients: A Mixed Methods Study."

our best interests at their core. In *Grief Dreams,* Tina J. Wray writes that nightmares help with all three stages of grief. She writes, "They can help us accept the reality of our loss. ... They help us work through the various feelings and emotions ... [and they] help us with the painful adjustment process as we learn to live in a world without our loved one." [68]

Nightmares help all people who must face the end of someone's life, whether we are ill ourselves, caring for someone, or living with the grief that comes with such loss. In all of these situations nightmares help us face the hard truths we might otherwise try to avoid. They help us understand and contain and eventually dissipate the strong negative emotions that threaten our equilibrium. They remind us forcefully of what we still want and need to resolve. And they mark with us our slow but eventual movement from grief and loss to a renewal of spirit.

Help Us Face Hard Truths

Like the woman who dreamed of doctors walking away from her, some dreams speak directly to the fears we can no longer ignore. Some grief dreams become nightmares when they replay the worst moments of a loved one's death. Often these dreams don't stick to known facts but instead home in on a moment that shows our strongest emotion about the death and how it feels now.

Susan McCoy, the trauma grief counselor, tells the story of a woman who went out looking for her son when he was late coming home from work, worried for him without knowing why. She came across the scene of a terrible acci-

---

68. Wray and Price, *Grief Dreams*, 120–121.

dent on her way, and the police had thrown a sheet over a body lying by the side of the road. All her anxiety came rushing up into her heart, and she was sure it was her son. The police told her to stay back with the other onlookers, but she had to do something. She took out her cell phone and called her son's number. She heard his phone start to ring underneath the sheet. At that point she passed out.

For months this poor woman dreamed of finding her son's body, seeing the sheet, and hearing the phone ring, the same dream over and over. Throughout her mourning she saw McCoy, who often just sat with her in silence at the enormity of her loss. This woman faced the worst moment in her life in those dreams, over and over, trying to make sense of a senseless tragedy.

Nightmares help dreamers understand traumas they have suffered, showing the same terrible events over and over again, until something inside the dreamer shifts, and the dreams begin to change. A bit at a time, this woman's nightmares helped her get used to the idea that this awful, incomprehensible event happened. Her nightmares helped her face her pain in increments, always with the option of waking up if the pain became too much to bear.

Sometimes the hard truths that nightmares make us face also contain a deeper truth about our very best selves. Wray includes the following dream in *Grief Dreams* from a man who watched his friend die of AIDS.

> *My early dreams of Elliot were scary hospital dreams. I would be back in the room with him, watching him sleep, terrified he would stop breathing. He was bald and emaciated,*

*the way he looked just before he died. Sometimes he would die
in the dream; other times, I would walk into the room and
find him dead with his eyes open. These dreams were terrifying, but they also reminded me that I was* there—*I stayed
even when I wanted to be anyplace other than that hospital—I was there until the end.*69

This man's dream reminded him of the worst moment in his
life. He was haunted by those dreams at first and wondered
why he was being taken back to such a hard moment. As
he held on to the dream, however, and played it over in his
mind, he was also reminded of his inner emotional strength
and determination to be at his friend's bedside. His dream
gave him a sense of pride about his ability to stay connected
with his loved one even in those terrible moments.

Help Us Hold Strong Emotions

In dreams people will sometimes revisit earlier times when
they felt under siege or in mortal danger. The dreamer wakes
with these memories of past traumas feeling fresh and raw, as
if they had endured the event all over again, and they wonder
why it has come back now. Dream expert Ernest Hartmann
suggests these nightmares are not solely reacting to the emotional turmoil of the earlier moment, but they are also connecting back to those times to help the dreamer. The dreams
are asking what helped the dreamer survive the last time and
what got them through those days, in the hopes they can remember their inner resources.

---

69. Ibid., 121.

Nightmares and bad dreams notify dreamers about fears and other disturbing emotions they might not otherwise notice. Like the dreams of the woman at the beginning of this chapter, nightmares and good dreams alike can bring our entire range of emotion into our conscious awareness, where we can find a way to meet them. The woman was overwhelmed by her negative feelings that threatened her self-image of a faithful person. The researcher helped her by "normalizing and validating her fear and anger about dying, while also reconsidering her stance that she should never allow herself to feel these emotions. By our final session... she had gained some important insights and increased self-acceptance." [70]

In chapter 2, I told about the caregiver who was overtired from all the work she was doing and then dreamed she was sinking on a life raft. She woke up feeling lost and alone. But the dream also helped her think again about how much she was doing and how tired she was feeling. Up until that moment she hadn't wanted help, and she had insisted on doing everything for her husband herself. I have met many caring spouses like her. They had never asked for help before, and they didn't want to need help now, even with the work piling up around them. They saw it as a failure of their competence and sometimes as a failure of their love. They scolded themselves, if they really loved their husband or wife, they would never feel this angry or frustrated. If they really loved their spouse they wouldn't want to waste a minute by not being together.

This woman's dream reminded her that she could get lost if she didn't take care of herself. It gave her the push she

---

70. Scott Wright, personal e-mail communication, January 2014.

needed to finally ask for help. The dream was tough, direct, and clear about her distress. It disturbed her just enough for her to accept help, which did her good.

Ernest Hartmann came up with a beautiful model for how nightmares help hold strong emotions after traumatic events. Nightmares are driven by strong emotions, but nightmares also help compare these strong emotions with the emotions we have felt in other stressful times. The dreams ask, is this the same anger, helplessness, hurt, frustration, or fear we have felt before? Or is it a little bit different? And how is it different this time? It is as if the dream state takes our worst fears and starts playing with the images, mixing and matching with any and all negative emotions we have ever experienced. The connections remind us of other traumas we've survived and of what we did then to bear the pain, until the original emotional charge is both weakened and spread out over decades of traumas large and small that we have successfully overcome.

Eventually all these dream connections help us understand the terrible event we face is just one more moment in our life, something we will eventually live through just as we survived traumas and hard times in the past. As the connections touch past moments of survival, our pain dissipates and we remember past moments of hope and resilience. As Hartmann points out, then "a new trauma or stress will be less 'singular,' less catastrophic, more familiar. ... In other words, we could say dreaming calms by cross-connecting."[71]

The dreams reflect the dreamers' inner strengths as well as the pain of the event, and that helps the dreamer find his

---

71. Hartmann, *Dreams and Nightmares*, 123.

or her own path to healing. One man was reminded of his loyalty and commitment to his friend despite his own fears. At the beginning of this chapter, a woman felt both jealous of her daughter and terrible guilt about feeling jealous. Over time, she found peace with these dreams, as she discovered she could have strong emotions without negating her deep love for her family.[72]

Remind Us of Unfinished Business

Just as dreams often express our relationships with others, nightmares bring to light broken relationships that need resolution, unkind feelings that need to be addressed, even final pieces of business that still need attention.

Tony is a hospital social worker who often helps people enter hospice care from the hospital. He knows entering hospice care is a life-changing decision for most people, and their dreams can reflect that. The nightmares people share with him mostly center on unresolved relationships. His patients dream of people who hurt them in the past or of estranged family members.

Nightmares prod dreamers into decisions and actions they may have been putting off. They wake from a dream of an estranged child walking away and know it is time to call and begin making amends. They have a dream in which they are unable to speak to their loved ones and they wake feeling compelled to write down their memories and family stories for future generations. At the beginning of this chapter, a woman dreamed her grandson was telling someone, "I don't remember Grandma." According to the researcher, "Then

---

72. Scott Wright, personal e-mail communication, January 2014.

the scene of that dream shifted so that she was witnessing her own funeral service at a Catholic church. She awoke frantic from this dream in the middle of the night and filled out some funeral-related paperwork that she had been putting off for months." [73]

In their own way, bad dreams tell people at the end of life they still have plans and hopes. They still have things to say, amends to make, and relationships to be healed. They still have responsibilities that only they can fill, and people who need them. What they no longer have is an unlimited future, which is a hard reality to face. Most of us put off doing things that feel uncomfortable, at least for a bit, but that is a luxury of the healthy. When people are nearing the end of life, matters become more urgent.

There is a consistent message underlying nightmares at the end of life that push dreamers to finish important matters. The message is the calm assertion that what they do even in their last days is important. What they say to their loved ones still matters and is still needed by their families, just as they are still needed and valued. Their dreams—good and bad dreams alike—give their last days relevance and purpose in a way nothing else can.

Mark Our Emotional Journey

Most nightmares have a marvelous fluidity to them. They shift and change over time, just as our emotions shift and change. They mark our emotional journey as we ready ourselves for death or for losing someone we love. Dreams re-

---

73. Ibid.

flect our emotions, so it is no surprise to know nightmares also respond to a new emotional landscape.

The woman who found her son's body by dialing his cell phone suffered through the nightmare of hearing his phone ring from under the sheet for nearly a year. After that, the dreams didn't come as often and gradually faded in their intensity as her grief slowly calmed. Three years after her son's accident, she had a dream that he was okay. In the dream he didn't speak, but he looked at her with love, then turned around and walked away. From that dream she finally got a sense that he was at peace and that she could be at peace, too.

The dreams marked her three-year emotional journey through grief, from the days when she could barely speak in the face of such unmitigated horror to the days when she was finally able to believe he was safe. She was able to move into the rest of her life, still connected with her son but in a new way that no longer tied her grief to his final moments of suffering. She doesn't know whether her dreams showed her how to heal or merely reflected her emotional journey, and she doesn't care. What matters is that her dreams kept her connected to her son until she could let him walk away in peace.

In 1995, researcher Mark Welman studied the dreams of twenty-one people from the time they began hospice care until they died. All together they offered 108 dreams marking a deeply emotional journey, from the terror of disintegration at the beginning to peace and wholeness at the end of life.

Nearly all of them had gut-wrenching nightmares at the beginning of the study. The very first dreams they described at the beginning of the study were merciless in pointing out to the dreamers that their bodies were disintegrating, being pulled apart and broken beyond repair, disappearing before their horrified gazes. These dreams left no doubt in the minds of the dreamers that their bodies were dying.

- *I was drowning in a pool of stagnant, rotting water. The stench was overwhelming. I hated it.* —Queenie

- *I was walking along High Street, carrying my handbag. Inside it I had a roll of film for developing. ... I knew that the film was very precious because it contained all of the scenes of my life. Then suddenly the whole bag caught fire and the film just evaporated in smoke. ... It felt as if my whole life was going up in a flash of smoke, and nothing was left of it.* —June

- *My arms and legs were being chopped off and into pieces by people who seemed to be cannibals, although I couldn't seem to be sure. ... I was in agony and terrified.*—Lawrence [74]

These first dreams clearly are nightmares. They gave the dreamers an unrelenting vision of their ultimate physical destruction, and many woke with pounding hearts. As von Franz wrote, nothing could be more clear in these dreams; the body deteriorates and dies, catches fire, and burns to ash that then evaporates, and there is nothing to be done about it. None of these dreamers found a way out of the dreams except by waking up. Other first dreams in this study included images of mechanical failures in cars, plane crashes, doctors walking away shaking their heads, funerals, and graves.

---

74. The dreams of Queenie, June, and Lawrence all come from Welman, *Death and Gnosis*, 255.

By their final dreams, however, all twenty-one people were dreaming of peace, wholeness, and meeting help for their next journey. As death approached their dreams shifted from reflecting their worst fears to illuminating their hope.

Queenie, who dreamed of drowning in stagnant waters, dreamed at the last of getting help from her deceased father. *"I was wandering around in some or other place. ... My father came and found me and led me away. I don't know where we were going, but I was happy to be going with him."*

June, who had dreamed her life pictures burst into flames, now dreamed of her parents coming to help her. *"I was in a beautiful chapel and found my parents [both deceased] praying for me. They seemed very much in love and looked happy and healthy. ... We all embraced and they said that they would always be there for me, just as they had when they were alive, and that we would soon all be together again."*

Lawrence's dreams transformed from the terror of being torn apart to a dream of absolute peace. *"I was holding a beautiful dove. I realized—even in my dream—that it was a symbol of peace ... that I'm ready to die now."*

Just as the first nightmares pointed out the body's decay to the dreamer in no uncertain terms, these final dreams were just as adamant that the dreamer's spirit would continue whole, untouched by the falling away of the body. Often in these final dreams an angel or a loved one comes to guide them into a new and beautiful place, and they feel peace, acceptance, and anticipation. There is light and an underlying, unshakable conviction that life continues beyond physical life.

In my own work I've mostly met people when they were nearing the final weeks of life. Despite the powerful benefits of hospice and its focus on living life well, most people still hesitate to accept hospice services until they absolutely must. Admitting to hospice means having to admit there is no more hope for treatment and cure, which is a difficult and painful decision for most people to make. Consequently, many people don't accept hospice services until the last few weeks of life, sometimes waiting until only days before their death.

Now I wonder if the comforting dreams they have shared with me reflect not just their preparation for end of life but perhaps also the timing of our meeting. I may very well have heard their final dreams of acceptance and peace without hearing of their earlier fight through the nightmares.

Researchers at the Center for Hospice and Palliative Care noticed the same thing in their recent study of the dreams of hospice patients. They heard a greater number of disturbing dreams from the people they visited in their homes—people who were still able to care for themselves independently—than they heard from people who were being cared for in the in-patient hospice unit. They wrote, "Those in the [home care] study often had unpleasant dreams characterized by a sense of tension. Theoretically, this may actually support the hypothesis ... that hospice patients less proximate to death ... were more likely to experience distressing dreams." [75]

Welman also worked with people who had just ended treatment at a cancer center and transferred their care to hospice. These people had just learned there was nothing more to be done to save their lives. They had to find a way to ac-

---

75. Wright, et al., "Meaning-Centered Dream Work with Hospice Patients: A Mixed Methods Study," 27.

cept the doctors' prognosis and turn to face something they had long been fighting against.

What is clear to me is the people in both studies were in a deep conversation with their dreams. They used their dreams to better understand their own hearts. Their dreams reflected their emotional journey of dying, and their dreams supported them on that journey. By acknowledging and accepting nightmares as a healthy reaction to the stress of dying, the dreamers learned from their dreams, which may have allowed the dreams to change over time.

How to Listen to Nightmares

Even the most terrible dreams can be responded to with the same simple and careful attention we have given to other dreams. Dreamers do well when someone they trust is willing to listen and to ask about the feelings and meanings they find for themselves. Michele Chaban, social work professor, asks the same questions of good dreams and nightmares alike. She focuses her questions on the dreamer's feelings and descriptions. "How did it unfold? How did you feel about it? What was it about?" If the dreamer doesn't know how to make sense of the dream, she is quick to say she doesn't know either. "I would help people wonder about it. Just sticking with the descriptors, asking about the experience, opening up with a state of wonder and awe, rather than knowing, and be willing to hold it."

There is no rush to analyze or dismiss the dream, just this careful, respectful observation. As Chaban says, "I teach people to hold [their dream]—not to analyze, not to judge, but just to describe. And in holding it and wondering about it, maybe even befriending what is monstrous that's coming out of you. Not having to tame it, but at the same time knowing that you're not holding it alone." This approach of listening without judgment helps keep dreams safe while respecting their powerful imagery. The monsters may remain monstrous, but they become our monsters, for our benefit somehow. These wild and untamed beasts are for our hearts alone.

Look for Insight

Monique Seguin, the licensed practical nurse, tells about an elderly woman in hospice who had a nightmare and was afraid to go to sleep. She asked the nurses for medicine to help her sleep without dreams, but she was still afraid. Seguin asked her if she would tell the dream, and she finally agreed. In her dream, she was trying to shove an ear of corn up a man's penis.

It was a painful, impossible, and disturbing image that set her on edge. She didn't want another dream like it and said she was considering never sleeping again, just to avoid it. Seguin asked the woman if the image reminded her of anything that had happened in the past few days. Yes! It reminded her of an old friend who had visited the day before, who had argued and refused to listen to her. Honestly, she said, her anger flaring again, arguing with him was like ... and then she laughed. *Oh.*

She suddenly realized her dream had given her the perfect image for her frustration. She understood what she had thought was a nightmare in fact was a good dream, responding to her feelings and faithfully mirroring them back to her, like any good friend. Instead of haunting her, this dream was giving her another way to understand her conversation with her friend. Her sudden insight lifted her fears about having another dream, and she was able to fall sleep without extra medication from then on.

Insight-oriented dream work is based on the idea that if we understand what the dream is trying to tell us, then we will no longer need another dream to give us the same message. Once this woman understood what her dream was showing her, she no longer worried about having another nightmare. With her new insight she could focus on her feelings about her friend directly.

Most dream work done today, whether it is offered in therapy or member-led support groups, is insight-oriented. People share their dreams and talk about what feelings they evoke, what messages they are hearing, and what it all means. As dream expert and author Jeremy Taylor calls it, dreamers are looking for the *aha!* of insight, that moment when the dream clicks in the dreamer's mind and heart and the dreamer exclaims, "Of course this is what it means!"

Listening to dreams for the light they throw on daily concerns helps many dreamers, but not all nightmares need a new insight before they can be resolved peaceably. Some nightmares push us to act on them, whether they are based on rational fears or not.

Act on the Dream

Acting on a dream can be as small as lighting a candle, praying, writing the nightmare down, or telling it to someone we trust. The action might not change our waking situation, but through the act we give respect to our hearts and to the dream as an inner source of meaning. When we take physical action in response to a dream, we are acknowledging its importance and, by association, the importance of our inner life.

Fiona Martins, the hospice nurse in Toronto, once worked with a woman who was caring for her husband. She had a repeating nightmare that her husband was accidentally buried alive. In each nightmare "they" were putting him into a casket and lowering him into the ground, but he hadn't died. He woke up and pounded on the coffin lid, but he couldn't get out, and she watched him die of suffocation.

This dream terrified the woman. There are just enough stories and folk legends told about such tragedies to make her wonder if this mistake might still be possible. She worried she might accidentally kill her husband by giving up on him too soon. When her husband did eventually die, she decided to heed her dream's warning. She waited nearly fourteen hours before reporting his death to anyone, which is a long time in the hospice world. She needed to make sure and triple-sure he was not struggling to come back.

When Martins arrived the woman tried to apologize, saying she felt foolish, but Martins helped her understand the importance of following that dream's warning. Martins told her, "You were comforted. You had him there for that long to make sure he didn't breathe again or do anything, so you knew that he truly was gone. And if it took you that time to be sure, then who am I to say otherwise? It's okay." Martins knew this woman's need to be sure came from her nightmares, and she understood such nightmares must be respected. "If my client needed her husband's body to remain in the house for that long, that's fine. You have to be very open to what is going to help family and not judge. You can't judge."

Martins respected the face value of the dream and didn't try to analyze it or make the woman see an underlying message. The end of a loved one's life is too important and too much a life-changing event in itself. Any kind of ostensibly helpful interpretation could have easily been seen as minimizing the very real fear this woman had of burying her husband too soon. Her dream told her to be sure, to be very sure, to wait until she was convinced nothing else was going to happen.

Martins supported this woman in what some might call a small act of irrational desperation, but others would clearly see as a ritual of assurance. It gave the woman a sense of peace and closure she might not have found otherwise. Imagine if the nurse had pushed her to deal with her fear more rationally by calling the doctor before the woman was emotionally ready. She might have had nagging doubts for years. A push to move past her fear, however kindly intended, could have added to her pain and grief.

Change the Dream

Sometimes people resolve nightmares by reimagining them, either while they are awake or from within a new dream. Reimagining a bad dream is like reimagining any waking life conversation that went wrong. We mutter and act out the distressing interaction over and over, changing our part until we feel sure next time we will be prepared. We'll know what to say. *What I could have said ... What I should have said ... Next time I won't be so timid [pushy, condescending, afraid]. Next time*

I will stand up for myself [listen more closely, be clear about my limits]. We know there most likely won't be a next time exactly like this one, but our rehearsing makes us feel more grounded in who we want to be. We practice and feel more sure about meeting the next challenging conversation.

Nightmares can sometimes be resolved using this same technique. It is less about gaining insight from the dream and more about reworking the dream just as we rework past conversations. Tony, the hospital social worker, sometimes asks dreamers to look at their nightmares of hateful or harmful relationships from the perspective of their current situation, much like Seguin asks her dreamers what the dream reminds them of now. He trusts the nightmarish visits from long-dead enemies are not there to hurt the dreamer but to help them deal with their present. Often he will ask them to imagine what a peaceful resolution to that relationship might look like. "The person [in your nightmare] is gone, but if there is something you can do now, what would help make it easier?" He encourages them to reimagine their relationships and practice saying out loud the words they need to say.

Our dreaming minds push us to recognize what we would most want to avoid and then give us images to help us sort through and understand our emotions. We don't have to enter into psychotherapy to understand our dreams. Most of the time simply having a friend who can listen to us sort through the images for ourselves can help. When we look closely at the nightmares that scare us, we often find friends in the guise of monsters and support in the guise of challenge.

Nightmares in times of grief provide an additional and often overlooked form of support. As painful as they can sometimes be, most nightmares help mourners feel connected to their loved ones. Mourners can feel further loss when their grief nightmares finally dissipate. No matter how painful those images were, mourners find the dreams give them one more chance to see and hear their loved ones again. Even nightmares with their bruising images can feel like a soul-level connection to loved ones.

Chapter Summary

Just as with preparation dreams and grief dreams, nightmares are not defined by any one specific image but by their emotional impact on us. Some of us can wake from dreams of destruction without a qualm, while others feel haunted by dreams that feature innocuous events. Like beauty, the power of nightmares lies in the eye of the beholder.

Nightmares play an important role in our lives. They help us face hard truths and give us a chance to hold strong negative emotions. They can remind us of what we still need and want to do, and they help us mark our emotional journey through grief.

Nightmares change when we gather the courage to face them. We can do this by engaging with them carefully. Some dreamers look for insight, others act on the dreams, and still others change the dream image in their imagination while they are awake. These are just a few ways we can connect with our nightmares as if they are ours. As if they are a part of us.

Talking about Dreams

- How do you respond to your frightening dreams?

- Have you ever told someone you trust about a nightmare? What happened to the nightmare after that conversation?

- Has a frightening dream ever spurred you to take some kind of action? What did you decide to do?

Chapter Eight

An Expanding Universe

This chapter is for all the experiences we can't technically call dreams because people aren't usually asleep at the time they happen. Even though they are not dreams, they are connected to the end of life and have much in common with important dreams at the end of life. The emotional power of these end-of-life experiences lies in the meaning they hold for us. The physical event might be quite small and ordinary, but the meaning of the experience can reverberate throughout a person's life. They are as important as our most intense, life-changing dreams. They are moments that hint to us we are not alone even as we live on without our loved ones. All we have to do is trust them. Unfortunately, this is not always easily done.

A few months after my father died, my stepmother, Judy, told me she'd had a strong feeling one night that my father was near her. For one intense moment she felt his touch, like he was hugging her, and knew he was watching over her and loving her even if she couldn't see him. It gave her a moment of immense peace in her grief. She felt loved and cared for. "I was so happy to have this feeling of his arms around me and feel his warmth and his breath."

She felt ... but then she stopped herself. "It wasn't real," she said. A well-meaning friend had explained to her how her grief had caused her to imagine my father's presence and that it only meant that she hadn't yet accepted the reality of his death. It was just wishful thinking. Now she reluctantly admitted to me that her feeling might have been only a momentary weakness and that she really did know better than to trust the peace she felt in that moment. She knew her life was not peaceful. Still, she held on to that moment of peace and comfort for weeks, alternately telling the story and disavowing it in the next breath, looking for validation while trying not to look foolish.

The end of life is a time when conscious awareness is in flux. Dying is a mind-altering experience, and those changes in perception can be as powerful and important to our healing as any experience in the rest of life. Life focuses down from all kinds of tasks and obligations to this one room, this one moment, then each moment becomes subtly charged with the urgency of impermanence; time becomes more precious because of its fragility. In these last blazing weeks and months, everyone—the person who is dying, the caregivers, the family, and the friends—all are invited to look more closely at what it means to be alive and conscious.

When we become more fully aware of our present moment our awareness expands. It takes in more details and makes more connections between our inner emotions and the world around us. We begin to notice patterns overlapping our personal lives and the physical world that we hadn't seen before, connections and patterns that nearly always bring comfort. These unusual experiences at the end of life fall roughly into five categories:

- Predicting the Moment of Death
- The Moment of Death Made Visible
- Final Goodbyes Across a Great Distance
- Small Events with Big Personal Meaning
- A Loving Touch, Familiar Fragrance

These connections have startled and confused people who weren't expecting to see them. When people don't know these moments are common human experiences, many hide them for fear of being seen as crazy.

Michele Chaban wanted to better support her clients when she worked with children who were dying. She taught her patients and families in palliative care to expect to see these new patterns and connections, and she helped them understand these experiences as both normal and helpful. Her explanations helped her clients and families hold on to a feeling of control and understanding with their inner lives.

> We gave people the language tools to talk about dying and death through relationship, dream states, imagining, through all the non-ordinary [awareness]. As people practiced recognizing and talking [about their] subjective experiences, they started to open up

to [unusual] perceptions and intuition. They found
these comforting rather than scary.[76]

Chaban's young patients and families felt comforted and intrigued because she had helped them understand what they
were experiencing. Over time, Chaban noticed families of patients on the unit were feeling comfortable enough to share
their unusual experiences with other families. "As they talked
to each other they noticed they might phone the nursing sta-
tion after a dream and hear the nurses tell them 'we were just
going to call you because something has come up.'" Because
Chaban had told them what to expect, the families found a
deep satisfaction in these connections, right in the midst of
their pain and fear.

Predicting the Moment of Death

In every nursing home, hospital, and hospice I've worked at,
nurses and social workers tell stories with awe about someone they knew who seemed to know or choose the moment
of their passing. One nurse described to me a nursing home
resident who was well enough to go home for a weekend
visit with her family. She had been steadily gaining weight
and strength over the previous two months and was looking
forward to going home. Then she did a curious thing.

Just before she left, she shook hands with all the staff and
thanked each of them for taking good care of her. The nurse
laughed. "We are going see you again in a couple of days," she
said, but the woman just smiled and shook her head. "I won't

---

76. Dr. Michele Chaban telephone interview in November 2012.

be coming back," she said. On Monday the family called to tell the staff she had died in her sleep early that morning.

Everyone was stunned. She'd had a great visit, seemed happy and energetic before going to bed Sunday night. She simply didn't wake up Monday morning. Unexpected to everyone, except to the woman who died. Staff at the nursing home asked each other, "How did she know?" for weeks as they retold this story.

Well sure, you might think, shouldn't we all know when our body is dying? I have worked in hospice a long time, and I can say with certainty that predicting a specific day to die ahead of time is not at all common. It's not the same as hoping to reach one more anniversary or a wedding. Most hospice doctors and nurses will refuse to predict the amount of time a patient has left, even when patients ask them, because they know there is no reliable method of predicting such a date. They tell a family the dying person has six months to live, and two weeks later their heart gives out unexpectedly. They tell a family the dying person cannot live more than a few days without water, and the family waits another agonizing week by the bedside. There are reliable signs that a person is within hours of dying, but being well enough to travel home for the weekend is not one of them. This is the usual state of affairs with the end of life.

So when someone does seem to know, we notice. Sometimes the visitors in visitation dreams bring a prediction that the person's time to die is approaching. The long-dead relative waiting to welcome them home with open arms reassures them the time is coming when they will be reunited. One woman had a visitation dream in which a local Catholic priest who had been killed in the 1960s came and comforted her.

She told the interviewer that Father Sean promised her she would die in exactly seven days. "He told me the end of the week. I am going to die in seven days." She felt calm then and patiently waited for her seven days to pass. During the next week she had two sudden medical events—a small stroke, a period of breathlessness—and each time she recovered. Exactly seven days after her dream, she died.[77]

It made the medical staff caring for her, who trust the power of modern medicine enough to devote their professional lives to it, question how a dream could know more about the body's timing of death than they could. It made them wonder for a moment not just about their patient but about Father Sean. Was his image a fragmented memory from decades earlier brought to light by the stress of her approaching death? Or did Father Sean actually visit her from an afterlife in which the date of this woman's death was not just predicted or guessed at, but known?

Stories like these bring an emotional relief to those in grief. The manner in which this woman's dream connected with her subsequent death gave her family and caregivers a new story about her life and death. It shifted the end of her life from a time of suffering from multiple medical crises into one that also included an unexpected calmness and serenity. It was a mystery to her family and all who cared for her during those last seven days, and it lifted her death from a

---

77. Pei C. Grant, Rachel M. Depner, and Scott T. Wright, personal communications, the Center for Hospice and Palliative Care, Buffalo, New York, September 2013.

pointless suffering into something more purposeful, as if she had been given a glimpse into (perhaps) a meaningful and loving universal spirit. The visitation dream didn't change her physical condition, but it added meaning, which helped calm the emotional suffering for her and her family.

The Moment of Death Made Visible

Sometimes family members see light in their loved one's room at the moment of death. The sun breaks through a cloud, the room suddenly brightens without anyone turning on a light, or a new light appears near the body of their loved one. People have described seeing strands of light leaving the body through the mouth, chest, head, and sometimes feet. It is as if the soul, or light, has become tangible for just a moment, coalescing into a form that is opaque and visible. One woman described both light and music in heavenly terms, only to have them vanish when the nurse touched her arm.

> *There was the most brilliant light shining from my husband's chest and as this light lifted upwards there was the most beautiful music and singing voices, my own chest seemed filled with infinite joy and my heart felt as if it was lifting to join this lift and music. Suddenly there was a hand on my shoulder and a nurse said, "I'm sorry, love, he has just gone." I lost sight of the light and music, I felt so bereft at being left behind.*[78]

---

78. Peter Fenwick, Hilary Lovelace, and Sue Brayne, "End of Life Experiences and Their Implications for Palliative Care," *International Journal of Environmental Studies* 64 (2007): 317.

These experiences are like waking visitation dreams, only this time the families are the ones who are caught up in their beauty. For a brief moment, the families see something wondrous and inexplicable. The light often brings a wash of warmth, love, and compassion before it disappears.

It is hard to know how often inexplicable light or music appears at the moment of death because so few people feel comfortable telling the story. In one study, researchers asked nurses at several different hospices about what they had witnessed at the end of their patients' lives, and nearly a quarter of them described seeing the dying person surrounded by light right at the moment of death. One person said, "When her mother was dying, this amazing light appeared in the room. ... The whole room was filled with this amazing light." [79]

More rarely still, visitation dreams can also become physically visible to people in the room. From the same study, the researchers spoke with a chaplain who witnessed such a visitation. He walked into a patient's room and saw what he could only describe as an angel sitting at the foot of the dying woman's bed. The woman was looking anxious, and when he asked her why she admitted she could see someone sitting on her bed and was worried it meant she was losing her mind. He told her he could see this person as well, and the woman relaxed. He later told the researchers:

---

79. Peter Fenwick, Hilary Lovelace, and Sue Brayne, "Comfort for the Dying: Five Year Retrospective and One Year Prospective Studies of End of Life Experiences," *Archives of Gerontology and Geriatrics* 51 (2009): 4. doi:10.1016/j.archger.2009.10.004.

She was a lady who had no family, which is why I said I wonder if somehow we are supplied with what we really need. She had no one. So somebody turned up to be with [her].[80]

When visitations are witnessed by a third person like this, they slide out of the category of a merely imagined event and into a category that as yet has no acceptable definition in modern Western culture. As rare as they might be, they push all involved to reexamine their beliefs about life and what comes after.

Final Goodbyes Across a Great Distance

Families and friends who are not at the bedside sometimes know the moment their loved one dies without being told. In times of war, these moments become more common. Families of soldiers wake from a dream of saying goodbye to their loved one and then find they died in those same hours. A mother wakes in the middle of the night to hear her son calling for her and then receives news a week later that he died that night. A father turns a corner and sees his son walking toward him, waving, before fading from sight, and comes home to find a military guard waiting to give him the news of his son's death.

Sometimes people feel their loved one's presence, as my friend Patricia did the night her grandfather died. She hadn't been able to travel back home to see him and found herself thinking of him on her drive home from work.

---

80. Ibid.

> As she paused at a corner before turning left, she had a
> sudden, strong sense that he was with her right at that
> moment, happy and loving her. She felt his warmth, and
> she was sure in that instant that he had died. Her mother's
> message about his death was waiting for her when she got
> home.

These visitations and dreams just at the moment of death
bring a sense of emotional belonging and connection to the
mourner. Mourners don't need any interpretation or additional meaning to help them know they were visited. They
understand they have received a rare gift and most hold on to
these moments as something to be treasured. The moments
express to them the dying person's desire to reach them at
such a crucial time, elevating their love to a power that transcends their physical death.

Small Events with Big Personal Meaning

Synchronicity is a term coined by Carl Jung, the Swiss psychiatrist and colleague of Sigmund Freud. The term describes
an ordinary event that suddenly gains intense meaning by its
connection to our emotional lives. To anyone else the events
look like random, inconsequential moments, but to the person who experiences one the event feels deeply connected to
an inner meaning. Synchronicities often happen in the moments immediately surrounding a death or in the months of
intense mourning that follow. They illuminate our emotional
connection to the world, and they help us feel held in the
midst of crushing loss.

A few months after her partner died, my friend Lee had one of these experiences. She was walking to her car one autumn afternoon and felt lonely and lost; she wished she could have a sign that Paula was all right and that she could survive this grief. She wasn't a strong believer in signs ordinarily, but there is nothing ordinary about grief. As Lee tells it:

I suddenly looked up and called out, "If only I had a sign, some way of knowing I'd be with you again, a promise." I don't know if my cry was out loud or in my heart, but as I looked up, a single perfect yellow maple leaf detached from its branch far above me and, in catching the last rays of sunlight, glowed as it began drifting gently back and forth toward me. I put out my hand like you would if someone was about to hand you something, and the leaf came and settled right on it. I didn't even have to reach.

It isn't unusual for a leaf to fall on someone who is walking underneath its tree or to watch one fall on a gust of wind. But Lee had been looking for a sign, and she had never before watched one particular leaf lift up into the wind and fall back to land gently in her hand. The leaf felt like an answer to her grief and longing, as if Paula had sent her one small moment of love she could hold in her hand once more. The leaf was hope and a promise that she was not traveling through her grief by herself.

Animals can also make unusual and highly meaningful appearances at the time of death. A wild songbird—the deceased person's favorite type of songbird—comes and sits on the windowsill outside the bedroom or somehow gets into the house. Eagles and hawks wheel in the sky above the hospital where a person who identifies with those birds lies dying. Several days after my friend Gene died, I dreamed he was sitting on the sidewalk across the street from my house, watching for me. The next morning when I started out for work I saw his cat sitting in the same spot and staring at me. I had given this cat to a neighbor a month earlier and hadn't seen it since. Now it sat on the sidewalk across the street, in the same place my friend had sat in my dream. I knew it was just a cat, and I knew it would be looking at my car moving slowly toward it, but for a moment my dream and the cat came together to form a last goodbye from my friend.

Signs and wonders are not confined to events in nature. Clocks have been known to stop at the time of a person's death, just like in the children's song "My Grandfather's Clock."[81] In the study of health care workers, nearly a third of them related stories of the watches and clocks of their clients' close family members stopping at the moment of death.

One person told me her watch had stopped at the moment her husband died. I saw her six months later ... and I said to her, "Have you still got the watch?" and she laughed. She said, "Yes, I bought a new one. I'm not going to have it repaired."[82]

---

81. Henry C. Work, *My Grandfather's Clock,* sheet music (New York: C. M. Cady, 1876).

82. Fenwick, Lovelace, and Brayne, "Comfort for the Dying: Five Year Retrospective and One Year Prospective Studies of End of Life Experiences," 7.

Health care workers have been startled to hear music playing in rooms after a patient's death and have been unable to find the source of the music.

Susan McCoy, the trauma grief counselor, hears about moments like this one from nearly every client she works with, and she helps her clients accept these moments for the healing messages they bring. "I can't think of a case that I've worked with where it hasn't [happened]."

These are important moments that help those in mourning feel a continuing emotional connection with the person who died. They seem to whisper to us that while death has separated us physically, there is something that lives on beyond death, something that can reach back to us with reassurance and love.

These small events with big meanings also make the life and death of the person we love seem necessary and important to the world at large. Their passing is so momentous that birds change direction midflight, wild (and domestic) animals turn and stare, and time stops, for just a moment. These events make us feel as if something greater than us notices this one great loss, the absence of this one life, as if our loved one mattered in ways we cannot comprehend. The enormity of these small moments is a comfort.

A Loving Touch, Familiar Fragrance

Susan McCoy told me about a client whose son was killed in a robbery of the store where he clerked. He was young and used to enjoy smoking marijuana, which she always hated. After his death she noticed every now and then her house would smell like marijuana again, as if he was in his room smoking. The woman decided the smell meant her son was talking to her, letting her know he was okay. McCoy supported her experience and interpretation and then had the chance to see (or smell) for herself.

> *I did a home visit and when I walked in there was no*
> *smell. Within no time at all there was a strong smell [of*
> *marijuana]. I was thinking there must be somebody else*
> *here and I asked, but she said, "No, I'm the only one here."*
> *And then it went away just as suddenly. I know marijuana*
> *is not a smell that goes away quickly. But here it was—*
> *instant on, instant off.*

The strong odor of marijuana spoke directly to this woman's relationship with her son. A smell that used to trouble her now took on a new meaning. Its sudden appearance and disappearance at odd times gave her a visceral sense of his presence and his humor that nothing else could touch. The smell told her that he was still himself and still connected with her.

To be clear, not every familiar smell carries a message from the deceased. I know I have caught an occasional whiff of my grandmother's perfume from years gone by, and each time it takes me back to her careful smile and folded hands. But I never thought she was visiting me. Each time I was in a crowd and could easily trace the scent to someone else walking by. The perfume was familiar enough to give me memories but not so unique that it felt like my emotional connection with her.

That is a very different experience from the mother in grief who caught a strong smell of marijuana in her own home with no one else present, a smell that appeared without cause and disappeared just as suddenly. The smell of marijuana did not act as a trigger for this woman's memory of some past moment—it acted instead as a form of communication between her and her son, between this world and the next where she now knows her son exists.

In the same way my stepmother, Judy, felt her husband's presence, and it gave her much-needed solace. It helped her through the worst days of her grief and gave her the courage to survive and remember him. She knows he is not physically here in her life anymore, and she doesn't wish for him to hang around in some ghostly form. But his presence in that moment held her again, stronger than memory, more vivid than longing, a response to her need that came from him, from outside of her.

Judy's story is achingly familiar in another way as well, in the negative reactions she heard from friends. I have talked with many people who wish they could trust their important dreams because those dreams brought such peace and eased their suffering, but they found they could not go against the judgment of friends and family who warned them about looking foolish, gullible, or irrational.

As McCoy notes, these moments are nearly always helpful in mourners' grief, unless the mourners are told by friends that the moment is bad or dangerous to their mental health. In fact, the only barrier to these moments McCoy can find is the consistent social pressure against them. Too many of her clients hear negative reactions from friends for daring to suggest they can actually smell their loved one's fragrance or feel them against their skin. "People will [tell the mourner], 'Are you crazy?' and 'They're dead. Just get on with life.'"

These moments often elicit more skepticism and questions than dreams do. Many people in Western culture already classify dreams as not real, so they don't feel provoked into the same kind of reflexive hushing when they hear about one. But these waking moments are more blatant about blurring the line between what is real out there in the world and what is imaginary here in our minds.

When I hear people rail against those who believe in things science can't prove to be real, I wonder what makes trusting a personal experience so terrible. I understand the frailties of memory and am glad our court system requires more than just memory to convict someone of a crime. But I don't know that this is a good argument against what many would call a profoundly moving personal—even spiritual— experience. With so much pain around the end of life, it feels like a second tragedy when people decide they cannot trust their own experience long enough to take any comfort from them. We give up too much when we require something as precious and deeply human as our capacity for love to conform to the rules of scientific research.

We have been taught that once a person is dead, he or she is gone. We have been taught to respect that firm line between life and no life, and to stay on our own side of that line as long as we can. In years past, grief experts used to encourage people to put the dead aside and get on with life as soon as possible, and most people still try to do just that.

When we turn away from our own experience, however, we add to our grief. We feel more lost because we are cut off from a vital part of ourselves. We end up feeling worse than if we felt nothing in the first place. To feel that comfort and then push it away because it might not be real enough makes the chasm of death seem even greater. Of the people who hold on to their experience, many worry, like McCoy's clients worry, that they will be seen as crazy if they admit they felt the presence of their loved one after death. Their joy and relief quickly turn into guarded secrecy that can become its own burden.

Fortunately, the stigma of our moments of connection is fading. Now grief experts are admitting many of us are stronger emotionally when we allow our dead an ongoing place in our lives. We can't put away the dead any more than we can put aside our hearts. They have formed our lives and will continue to form our futures in unexpected ways.

Several researchers call these post-death encounters "continuing bonds," meaning the experience helps people hold and strengthen their emotional bonds with the person who died. As researchers Nadine Nowatzki and Ruth Kalischuk report:

> The encounters profoundly affected the participants'
> beliefs in an afterlife and attitudes toward life and
> death, and had a significant impact on their grief.
> Finally, post-death encounters had a healing effect on
> the participants by contributing to a sense of connect-
> edness with the deceased.[83]

---

83. Nadine R. Nowatzki and Ruth Grant Kalischuk, "Post-Death Encounters: Grieving, Mourning, and Healing," *Omega* 59 (2009): 91–111.

All of these moments point to the possibility of an emotional, and perhaps spiritual, connection that holds fast long after the moment of a loved one's death. They are tiny events with outsized meaning attached to them, meanings that far outstrip the physical trappings of what happened and who saw what. Their impact lies in their meaning as defined and discovered by the people who witness them.

I think these moments do more than simply give us a moment of peace in the midst of our grief. They ease our question of whether our loved one is finally out of pain. They lift our guilt and our fear of being abandoned. They reassure us of the strength of our emotional connection by showing us how it transcends our physical separation. They reveal the strength and durability of our love for each other. They tell us again we are loved and our love still matters to the person who died. They tell us we can remain connected to those who have died and that this emotional connection with our loved ones transcends the physical separation of death. All of this is to say they bring us healing.

Chapter Summary

Facing the end of life, whether that life is our own or that of someone we love, can be both terrifying and profound. When our hearts are stretched beyond what we once thought we could endure, we sometimes find that the universe expands along with us. We see a light surround our loved one or hear music at the time of their death. Clocks stop, animals pause to watch, and everything—anything—can become a sign, a final message of love, or a moment of deep connection with those we have lost. These moments can bring healing if we allow them in.

There are times when the earth feels like nothing more than a giant rock orbiting the sun, an accident of the cosmos spinning in an empty, cold, and meaningless universe. And then there are the moments like these when we are shaken out of our empty spaces and pushed to see the patterns of meaning and connection swirling around us. For one glorious, heart-yielding moment the universe is infused with meaning, saturated, and we stand breathless and uncertain, transfixed in its light.

Talking about Dreams

- Have you ever had an experience you couldn't explain at the end of someone's life? What happened, and how did it affect your grief?

- Has anyone told you about an unusual experience of theirs? How did you respond?

- These end-of-life experiences have no easy explanations, and at the same time have a profound emotional impact on the people who experience them. How do you make sense of them?

Part Two:
How to Build a Dreaming Life

The first part of this book explored some of the ways dreams can help you and your family when someone faces the end of life. Dreams can help begin much-needed conversations, prepare people who are ill for an unknown future, and comfort those in grief. They can only do all of this, however, if you listen to them. If you don't remember your dreams or talk about them, if you never act on their suggestions or listen for their insights, then their potential to help you will be limited.

Part 2 looks more closely at how you can cultivate a richer partnership with your dreams. Chapter 9 can help you remain open, curious, respectful, and unknowing in the face of someone else's dream. You don't have to understand Jungian archetypes or Freudian theories in order to help; you only have to listen and trust the dreamer can make sense of the dream for him or herself.

Chapter 10 gives suggestions on how to better remember your own dreams. How you respond to your dreams now can impact the usefulness of your dreams. If you can cultivate a stronger relationship with your dreams, they will become more coherent and more relevant to your daily life.

Finally, the epilogue considers how dreams and dream appreciation fits within the larger questions of human dignity and what makes life worthwhile.

Chapter Nine

How to Listen to Dreams at the End of Life

My friend Peggy is a retired hospice social worker who has an active personal dream life. She trusts her dreams and likes thinking about them while she is awake, but in all the years she worked with the dying she never once thought to ask her clients about their dreams.

Her work was primarily geared to psychosocial assessment, setting up needed services, and occasional counseling. Asking about dreams seemed to her a bit dangerous. What if she inadvertently opened up emotional issues she couldn't resolve? She said, "If I ask about a dream, what do I listen for? If they tell me a dream, how do I assess it for problems? Where is the protocol, the interventions to help people do their dreaming better?" As a health care professional and an expert in end-of-life care, she felt inadequate to advise her clients about their dreams, which made her wary of asking about dreams in the first place.

Peggy's concerns are echoed by many people, both within and outside the field of health care. The health care colleagues I've talked with over the years—chaplains, nurses, counselors, social workers, and doctors—have nearly all felt inadequate to the task of listening to dreams. Doctors and nurses especially are accustomed to their roles as medical experts, meaning they provide answers for their clients rather than ask their clients for answers. They feel vulnerable when confronting an experience they cannot control, explain, or treat. Without a standard of practice to follow, most feel painfully out of their area of expertise.

I have found some of these same concerns outside of health care as well. Even without a professional obligation to stay within a certain medical practice, most people in Western culture shy away from asking about dreams. Most of us know how to dream ourselves, but listening to the dreams of someone else feels beyond the scope of our daily expertise. What if I listen to my friend's dream but I don't know what it means? Or worse, what if I think I do know what it means but he denies it?

Three Revolutions in Dream Work

Our feelings of inadequacy in the face of dreams may come from the very people who brought dreams back to the attention of Western culture in the first place. Sigmund Freud initiated the first revolution in dream work when he introduced a scientific approach to dream analysis. Freud described dreams as unconscious fantasies, unfulfilled wishes, and repressed urges that dreamers will not allow themselves to consciously acknowledge. With his new method, called psychoanalysis, dreams could at last be interpreted systematically. Doctors could be trained to help clients understand their unconscious drives, emotions, and impulses through their dreams.

Carl Jung extended this first revolution by building on Freud's idea of unconscious urges with his own theories that retold the story of dreams as our modern connection to great and ancient spiritual forces still at work in human souls. Where Freud used dreams to search out mental unwellness, Jung followed dreams into the world's soul, what he called the *collective unconscious*. Jung reintroduced modern Western culture to the power of dreams and their potential to connect modern dreamers to the greater mysteries of life.

They both revealed unsuspected depths hidden in the most ordinary dreams—the dark, repressed impulses of Freud and the archetypal forces of Jung. Both Freud and Jung were educated in the nineteenth century with its reverence for ancient Greek and Roman mythologies, and they used those mythologies to teach the general public about dreams.

Freud and Jung also each introduced strict rules of en gagement with dreams, putting dream interpretation into the hands of proper analysts who had years of education and training, as befitted a new science of the mind. It didn't take long for ordinary dreamers—especially those without a classical education—to feel incompetent to engage with dreams on their own. People began wondering if there was something inherently dangerous about dreams, as if one dream or one dream interpretation could do harm to the dreamer.

In the 1960s Montague Ullman, a psychiatrist at Maimonides Hospital in New York, created the second revolution in dream work. He developed a simple method of group dream exploration that people could use without a mental health professional's guidance. His approach is based on three main points:

- Respect for each dreamer as the sole judge of what the dream means for him or her
- The importance of a group for providing multiple perspectives
- Emotional safety and confidentiality for the group [84]

This approach opens a wide range of new ideas to the dreamers without obligating the dreamer to accept someone else's interpretation. It gives dreamers room to consider new meanings without forcing them to accept any one interpretation. It also gives listeners a chance to listen to the dream as a story that speaks to their own experience directly. With each dream listeners have an opportunity to explore their own personal response to the dream's message.

Ullman's work was revolutionary in its own right, bringing dream interpretation out of psychiatric consultation rooms and back into the hands of all dreamers. His dream group method gives people a chance to meet with others who are interested in exploring dreams in depth.

Ullman's work has inspired a new generation of professional dream workers who teach their own version of the Ullman method. Reverend Dr. Jeremy Taylor has done more than most to popularize Ullman's work and broaden its use to new contexts. In his book *Where People Fly and Water Runs Uphill: Using Dreams to Tap the Wisdom of the Unconscious*, Tay-

---

84. Montague Ullman, "Dream Work and the General Public," *Psychiatric Journal of the University of Ottawa* 12 (1987): 103–108.

lor shows how group dream work can help in community development, with people living in prisons, and with theological students.[85] Taylor and other dream work experts have opened schools and programs designed to train new dream work facilitators.

Today you can attend a dream work group or dream class in nearly every city. The insights that come out of these groups has encouraged people to start dream work groups in a range of settings, including retirement communities,[86] cancer treatment centers,[87] churches, and schools.[88] Dream groups offer emotional support to dreamers, and many develop over time into social networks. Some groups meet once a week for years; others meet for just a few months before disbanding.

Over the decades dream groups have expanded the ways in which they explore dreams. In addition to sharing the dream through storytelling, some dream groups encourage people to draw their dream images. Others teach people how to act out the different parts or imagine themselves as every single object, person, or animal in the dream. People in dream groups learn to reimagine important or distressing dreams and give them a new ending. All dream work groups increase a sense of belonging as people share private parts of themselves and hold gently the private lives of others.

At the end of life, however, such in-depth work becomes less doable for people who are ill and incapacitated. Often

---

85. Jeremy Taylor, *Where People Fly and Water Runs Uphill: Using Dreams to Tap the Wisdom of the Unconscious* (New York: Warner, 1992).

86. Rachel Aubrey, "Dream Sharing in a Retirement Community," *Dream Time* 23 (2006): 12–41.

87. Lyons, *Dreams and Guided Imagery*.

88. Taylor, *Where People Fly and Water Runs Uphill*.

people don't have the energy or interest to maintain such a project. Dream group facilitators have rightly decided this type of dream work too often takes more energy and time than the person can give.

What we need now is a way to hang on to our dreams for the benefits they clearly bring, without taxing limited strength or patience. Our dreams are too important a source of comfort, hope, and courage at the end of life to just let them go. What we need is one more change—a fourth revolution—in the way we think about and interpret dreams.

Just as we have let go of the need for a Freudian analyst to help us understand our dreams, we may now be ready to let go of the absolute need for in-depth, insight-oriented interpretations. There are times in life, such as at its very end, when in-depth interpretations are no longer necessary. When time and patience and physical energy have all run short, dreams become more direct and to the point. They need less interpretation and "work" to find a meaning that holds the dreamer. They become more of an invitation to connect the dreamer back to his or her life.

William A. Cramond, a Freudian analyst who worked in a general medical hospital in the United Kingdom in the 1960s, wrote an article in 1970 questioning the need for traditional analysis on dreams of people who were dying. This was startling because Freudian analysts of that time were the first to say dreams need a skilled clinician to interpret their deeper symbolic meanings. Dr. Cramond worked during the peak of psychoanalysis's popularity, and he was well versed in classical dream interpretation. When he listened to the dreams of people who were dying, however, he found no need to press them to move past the surface images. Instead, he saw that dreams at the end of life brought comfort and hope at first glance.

He tells of one hospital client who was too frail to be discharged and who absolutely refused to acknowledge her approaching death. As she weakened she became depressed and was often agitated, but she refused to talk about what was happening to her. Dr. Cramond wondered how she was going to prepare herself for her final moments.

Then she began talking about a series of dreams in which her mother-in-law and brother, both long dead, came to visit her. She was surprised to see them. The psychiatrist refrained from encouraging her to make connections between their sudden appearance and her illness. Instead he asked her to tell him about them, and as she did she visibly relaxed. She described their kindness to her and the way they reached out to care for her when times were difficult. She said she had always felt close to them, and as she talked about them, she found a new peace. Dr. Cramond never did interpret her dreams, noting instead, "by simply telling of her happy memories of the two who had gone before she was given some relief and was able to adjust within her limited resources to her dying." [89]

This woman's dreams didn't talk to her about dying. They helped by reconnecting her to the people in her life who loved and cherished her. When she could talk about her memories to a willing listener, she found her own peace. Her depression and agitation lifted in part from the dream and in part from her

89. William Alexander Cramond, "Psychotherapy of the Dying Patient," *British Medical Journal* 3 (1970): 391.

remembering out loud those important, loving relationships. She found comfort in the telling of her dream as much as from the dream itself.

Researchers who have looked at end-of-life dreams in the past two decades all have noticed something similar—the comfort and message of these dreams lie more often in the surface images than in any indirect associations they may carry. Dreams at the end of life may carry symbolic meaning but more often they speak directly to the life of the dreamer, for good reason. When waking life becomes one long emotional and physical challenge, our dreams respond with images that speak directly to that challenge.[90] As a result, even those clinicians who had planned on helping their clients interpret end-of-life dreams often found themselves stepping back instead. The dreams' messages often are so clear there is no burden on the listener to uncover hidden meanings.

Dreams can help all who remember them, whether they wake with epic sagas running through their heads or have captured only a single image. All we need to do is listen and allow the dreamer room to make sense of their own experience. Listeners can help best when we allow the people we love to simply talk about their dreams and how those dreams affect them.

Telling a dream may need no more than a few minutes' time before the attention of all involved turns back to a newly enriched waking life. Inviting people to tell their dreams can

---

90. Scott T. Wright, Pei C. Grant, Rachel M. Depner, James P. Donnelly, and Christopher W. Kerr, "Meaning-Centered Dream Work with Hospice Patients: A Mixed Methods Study," 25. "The high salience of waking-life concerns related to dying may account for the preference of waking-life interpretations."

be as direct as "Do you dream?" or as casual as "How are your dreams these days?" Telling a dream often needs only one or two sentences, such as "Good. I dreamed of an old friend last night whom I haven't seen in years," or "Really boring. I dreamed I was taking pills all night."

These are not lengthy dream reports. They carry few details, just a brief overview of its main action, emotion, or message. Dreams such as these can still open a path into new conversations. A dream of an old friend can lead to memories of that person and of what life was like for them way back when. A dream of taking too many pills can lead to a conversation on how they are taking care of themselves, or how they feel about all the pills, or what their relationship to medicine was before all this.

Sometimes I ask dreamers, "How did you feel in the dream?" or "How does it relate to your situation now?" Our conversations turn out to be less about the dream images and more about what the dreams point to, such as the particulars of their lives or their ways of walking through the world. We don't need the dreams to do more, but without the dreams I might never have seen the rising frustration with pills or heard about the dreamer's friends.

The dream opens us into a richer version of daily life in which emotions and spiritual beliefs rise in importance to match the running list of tasks we keep in our heads. The dream lets us talk about what life is like, instead of how the weather is shaping up or the errands they still need to run. And sometimes the dreams take us into the heart of dying. Here is an example, taken from many such conversations during my job.

A man tells me, "I don't remember much. I was standing in
a line all night and nobody was moving. It was frustrat-
ing." How do you feel about it now? "I'm kind of wonder-
ing what the line was for." He pauses. "I know I'm stand-
ing in line now, but I don't know where I'm going."

That's all it takes. We have moved from the dream into a question he has been pondering, about where he is heading. And
even here I will not make assumptions about what he means. I
will wait and let him explore this dream as he wants. He might
want to talk about waiting for some important event with his
family. Or he might be wondering where he is going after this
life ends and whether or not there is a Heaven. The dream
might lead him to an emotional settling with his illness and approaching death. This simple dream fragment gives a story, an
action that helps the dreamer put the deeper part of his emotional life into words. He doesn't need to explore the dream
any further than that to find its benefit.

How to Listen to Dreams

Listening to dreams at the end of life needs no dream-
interpretive skills or knowledge. Only one of the health
care professionals I interviewed had any special knowledge
of clinical psychology or dream theory. Tallulah Lyons—
the daughter of Jerry in the introduction—facilitates dream
groups for people living with cancer. Other than Lyons,
the people I spoke with are nurses and chaplains and social
workers, and none of them had studied dreams beyond a few
hours in their respective programs. Most wouldn't recognize
a dream about ancient Greek or Roman gods if one came up

and kissed them on the cheek. They had only one thing in common—they had found a way to listen to the dreams of others.

The skill these people share is the ability to listen. They share the strong belief articulated by Jeremy Taylor, that dreams come for our benefit and will speak in a language we can understand, so these professionals don't feel a need to teach or interpret the dreams. They trust the dreamers will be able to make sense of their own dreams. They know every dream is a form of communication, and they trust people will tell their dreams to make a point, to start a conversation, or to share what they feel and think about something important. They let the dreams lead them to what matters most to their clients at that moment.

They do take it upon themselves to open the conversations about dreams, which is a skill that can be taught. Through my interviews I found they all used the same three steps to encourage people to tell their dreams. Despite some hesitations and fears of doing the wrong thing, they all discovered these three steps helped return dreams to the conversation:

- They make dreams safe for telling.
- They consistently invite people to tell their dreams.
- They listen without adding their own interpretations.

When they follow these three steps as a listener, they give their clients room to share and to appreciate their own dreams. They acknowledge the importance of the dream and the dreamer's ability to make sense of it. This in turn helps them acknowledge and respect their clients' inner selves with their inherent dignity.

Make Dreams Safe for Telling

At first glance the question of creating a safe space in which people can tell their dreams might seem unnecessary. We all have become so accustomed to keeping our dreams private we rarely think about the potential social consequences if we were to talk about them, but those consequences loom when dreams become powerful. When people have dreams powerful enough to change their lives, as so often happens at the end of life, they often keep those dreams hidden. The health care professionals I interviewed all remarked on their patient's caution around telling their dreams, sure their perspective would be looked upon with disdain and outright dismissal. As Michele Chaban notes, "[Patients and families] hide [their dreams] because they're afraid that somebody's going to think that they're daft and psychiatry is going to be called in."

Chaban taught her young clients and their families to expect and embrace the different kinds of "dreams and dream states, hallucinations, senses of others who have died coming back for you—all are within a very normal realm of dying." By talking about these states early and emphasizing their importance and helpfulness, Chaban helped her clients and their families accept their experience as real.

The health care professionals needed first to reassure their clients that any dreams they shared would be treated with respect. Only then were clients willing to risk their dreams. To be asked about dreams without that fear of judgment, in a way that recognizes the strength and wildness of dreams, can feel thrilling, scary, and ultimately freeing to the dreamer.

The health care professionals I interviewed created a safe space by stressing their own belief that dreams are normal, common, natural, and have something worthwhile to offer. They promise the dreams will be treated with respect with their words and actions. In many ways, they normalize dreams for their clients. Some do this by sitting down and talking about the importance of dreams in general.

Jay Libby, the hospital chaplain, finds he is often called to reassure his clients who have had intense visitation dreams. He reassures them that such dreams are both natural and real before moving into a discussion about what meaning the experience has for them. His experience echoes the work of researchers who talked with nursing home staff in the United Kingdom. The researchers found "often patients simply need to be reassured that their experiences are quite normal and happen to many people, most of whom find [this reassurance] comforting." [91] The two grief counselors, Phyllis Russell and Susan McCoy, also find many of their clients bring up the topic of dreams in a general way before telling their own dreams. Russell and McCoy respond by talking to their clients about dreams as a useful and respectable tool for mourning. All of this encouragement helps lessen the fear and confusion that sometimes happens when people don't have an explanation for a vivid personal experience.

---

91. Fenwick, Lovelace, and Brayne, "End of Life Experiences and Their Implications for Palliative Care," 320.

Invite People to Tell Their Dreams

Fenwick, Lovelace, and Brayne, the same UK researchers cited above, studied the visitation dreams, sudden peaks in lucidity, and moments of peace and comfort that often come in a person's final hours.[92] They interviewed nurses and attendants who had secondhand stories of such "death-bed phenomena" from their patients and families. Most of the nurses privately admitted they believed such things to be true, but they didn't initiate conversations about dreams with anyone—not their patients, families, or colleagues—and they noted it was rare for patients to bring up the subject.

When asked why they thought patients didn't tell them about their experiences more often, they responded with a list of perfectly rational concerns. Patients might feel embarrassed or worry about distressing their families with crazy talk. Some patients didn't speak English as a first language. There is not enough privacy on the inpatient units. Many are made too drowsy from pain medication. But a few nurses also admitted that perhaps patients didn't share their dreams more often because no one asked them.

This silence around dreams begins when we are young. We grow up in relative isolation with our dreams, keeping them tucked away in a private space, hidden from all but a trusted few. Nobody asks about them and over time we learn to move talk about dreams into the category of social taboo. In Western culture, we learn dreams are not to be discussed or trusted.

---

92. Brayne, Farnham, and Fenwick, "Deathbed Phenomena and Their Effect on a Palliative Care Team: A Pilot Study:" 17–24.

Last year I had an opportunity to talk with children (ages three to seventeen) and their parents about dreams at a community center. At my table I invited the children who wandered by to tell me about their favorite dream and then draw a picture of it on a large piece of butcher paper.

More than a hundred children crowded around my table over the next three hours, describing and drawing dreams of all kinds. Many of their parents were surprised by their children's dreams. They shook their heads and said, "I didn't know you dreamed that." I heard a few parents say, "I didn't know you remember your dreams." Some parents added their own dreams to the picture, but most stood back in surprise at the vividness and complexity of their child's dreams. I hoped these conversations might spark in parents a new curiosity and appreciation for their children's inner lives and maybe encourage them to ask about dreams in the future.

The invitation to tell a dream, whether it is casual or more formal, signifies interest and a level of respect for dreams. The invitation says a dream can be an important, noteworthy event.

Some of the health care professionals I interviewed ask about dreams or about their clients' sleep on a regular basis. Their questions are direct and friendly, emphasizing again the natural place dreams hold in daily life. *How are your dreams? Do you dream? Would you like to tell me a dream? What is your dream life like? Have you been dreaming about your loved one?* They ask consistently, folding the question in with all their other questions on each visit. They invite people to tell their dreams in such a routine and nonthreatening manner that their clients respond with the same eagerness I saw at the community center when I asked children and their parents to share their favorite dreams. I often asked my clients, "How are your dreams these days?" and found this general question allowed people to respond in any way that felt safe for them.

Monique Seguin, the licensed practical nurse, found that inviting dreams was as easy as adding a few questions to her evening routine "Do you dream?" or "How are your dreams?" And then before saying goodnight, she wishes them, "Have good dreams."

Fiona Martins, the palliative care nurse, is more concerned with dreams that get in the way of sleep, so she asks about their sleep first. "I don't bring up dreams exactly, unless they're not sleeping well. If they say 'I can't sleep because I'm having bad dreams' or 'I'm waking up because of the dreams,' then we talk about it." Other nurses on inpatient units have found that simply asking, "How did you sleep last night?" as part of routine care is often seen as an invitation to talk about dreams.

Listen without Interpreting

The people I interviewed who are most comfortable with their clients' dreams make a practice of listening without adding any interpretation. Each one of them spoke of the impossibility of interpreting accurately someone else's dream. They recognized they had no training in dream interpretation, which helped them all take great care in keeping their own interpretations to themselves. Their lack of training made them less tempted to add their own ideas about the dream, which in turn made them ideal listeners.

Listening without interpreting might seem like a small gesture of politeness, but it is the most important point of listening to the dreams of people at the end of life. People at the end of life have more than enough people explaining their illness, examining their bodies, or giving them medicines they don't understand. They don't need another expert explaining their dreams to them as well. They need someone who will remember they are still the undisputed expert in their life in at least one area.

Listening without offering interpretation offers the dreamer a new level of respect. The clinician respects that the person who is telling the dream will know best what to share and is able to make his or her own sense of the experience. This respect, so simple to give, can have an enormous impact. The whole person becomes visible again. They are not simply their illness or their dream; they are the person who makes sense of their own life, which respects their dignity as a human being.

For the precious time of a dream's telling, the patient becomes the storyteller and bringer of dreams. We have seen throughout this book the ways dreamers bring a true gift to their families when they tell a dream. Often the dreams reveal the inner complexity and dignity of the dreamer in their final days. The families, in turn, recognize in their loved ones their capacity for love, change, and integrity. As Michele Chaban notes from her work in a pediatric hospice, "If you give people place and space for their own experience rather than trying to fit them within the medical model ... [you can see] the rich experience of what dying can be for people." The dying person becomes sage and teacher. Sharing dreams is something the ill person can do right up until they can no longer communicate.

The people who learned to ask their clients about dreams all ask simple questions to help clients make sense of their dreams. They ask "How did you feel in the dream?" "How does it feel now?" "What does it remind you of?" "How do you make sense of it?" They trust the dreamers to discover their own connections to the dreams.

Michele Chaban treated all her young dreamers with care. "I would ask them questions like, 'What do you think that was about?' and 'How did you feel when you had that experience?'"

Susan McCoy, the trauma grief therapist, responds to intense grief dreams about the deceased with appreciation and the invitation to explore. "I'll say, 'Tell me more,' and 'How is that for you?' 'What's most important for me to know now?' and 'Isn't it wonderful that this is part of your new way of connecting, a new way of being in relationship with that person?'"

These health care professionals trust the dream images will help deepen conversations with their clients about life, relationships, hope, fears, what makes a good life, or whatever comes up, just as it did in my own work. They all see the dream as working on behalf of the dreamer to help them approach the end of life with as much resolution and peace as they can find.

You Can Listen to Dreams

At this point you might still be thinking, *Yes, but these people are all professional caregivers. Who am I to listen to someone else's dreams? I haven't read all the dream dictionaries. I don't know what unconscious impulses lurk beneath the surface. I haven't read*

enough Jung or Freud or Ullman. How can I possibly add anything
of worth to the dreams of my loved one? You are not alone with
these worries. Many people feel inadequate when it comes to
listening to the dreams of other people. Many experienced
dream workers also feel anxious at the beginning of each
new group. Then they remind themselves they are not supposed to know everything, and they relax.

What is difficult to remember is how easily this worry
can be answered. You probably can't analyze the dreams, and
that very fact makes you the ideal listener. You will be less
tempted to jump in with your insight or try to cleverly steer
the dreamer in a certain direction with your questions. The
longer you can remain open and curious about their experience, the more help you will be.

Most dreams at the end of life need nothing more than
recognition and acceptance. If you can be the audience, then
the dreams will take care of themselves. The dreams will
take care of the dreamer, just as the dreamer gives meaning
to the dream. The dreams might take care of you as well, giving you a closer relationship with the person you love.

All you need are the three steps we've been talking about.
Make a dream safe to tell by showing your interest. Invite
dreams by asking about them. Listen without interpretation.
You don't have to be a health care professional or have any
training in dream interpretation. Being someone the dreamer
loves and trusts will help both of you tell and listen to dreams.
Remember that dreams and their meanings ultimately belong
to the person who dreams them. Ask simple questions, such as:

- What happened next?

- How did you feel in the dream?

- What do you think it means?

- What does it remind you of?

- How do you feel about it now?

That is all you need to open a door to someone's dreams. Ask, and then listen for the answers. Remain open to whatever story the dreamer tells and whatever meaning the dreamer finds in it. If they aren't sure what a dream means, if they shake their heads and say it's all nonsense, then accept the nonsense of it. Shake your head along with them and marvel at the mystery, and then invite the next dream. The longer you can sit with the dream without rearranging it to fit into your own ideas of what a dream should be, the more room you leave for its meaning to reveal itself.

If you are worried such an invitation to tell a dream will lead to questions you can't answer, remember you are listening to someone you love and know, and someone who loves and knows you. Very few people will assume you have suddenly developed the skill to do a complete psychoanalysis of their dream. Most people will know how to tell their dream within the space you have to listen, just as we know when and how to talk about any other aspect of our personal life in the space available.

If by some chance you do have someone ask you for your interpretation, you can always shrug your shoulders. If they want to know if you have studied dreams, you can say no without losing face—very few people outside of psychology have studied dreams to any extent. Even psychologists no longer study dreams in the same Freudian/Jungian manner. If your loved ones want to know why you are so interested in their dreams, you can point out that we all dream, even when everything else falls away. You can say you trust we all dream for our own benefit and that you believe some dreams—perhaps most dreams— can be helpful. Practice saying, "I don't know what it means. I think only you can know what the dream means to you."

The truth is dreams can be appreciated on any level we want. We can always delve into the meaning of ancient symbols and hidden metaphors when we have the time and energy for such exploration, but we don't have to. Dreams can be useful at their surface as well as in their depths. A man might tell me, "I had a flying dream last night—it was great!" and then spend fifteen minutes talking about when he used to fly planes or what it was like in his dream seeing the ground from up high and feeling the wind against his face. We could look at the symbolic meaning of dream flight or the history of flying dreams or what flying means in other cultures, but it isn't necessary. Some dreamers will be satisfied with reveling in the physical sensation—and the freedom—of flight. They might need nothing else other than to tell the adventure, just as if that experience is important in itself.

When you can listen without jumping to explain it or make it fit, you will be giving a gift of genuine presence. Sit with the unfamiliar images and allow the dream room to breathe in the open space between you. Help your loved ones listen to their own dreams with an open attitude, trusting the meaning and connections will be apparent soon enough.

Listening to dreams allows a kind of integration, a merging of our inside and outside realities. Dreams bring to our surface old emotions, new life questions, and memories of our successes and failures, our regrets and pride, our loves, our loved ones, the meaning and purpose for our life. This is soul work, perhaps the most important work of all at the end of life. These emotions and questions and hopes are part of us, and our dreams give us a glimpse of our inner workings.

Listening to dreams reminds us all again of the inherent dignity of the person who is ill, something that can get lost among the many essential caregiving needs. People at the end of life often are nudged into passively trusting the authority of the doctors and nurses. Dreams allow them to be in charge again, first inside the dream and then again when they tell it to someone who appreciates it. They are in charge when they explain its meaning or declare it has no meaning at all.

More than feeling in charge, telling a dream allows the dreamer to give something of value to the family. It restores dignity by showing all involved that the dreamer has something to offer, something that will help the family through this crisis. That is true whether the dreamer is the person who is ill, the spouse, or the youngest child.

Dreams work best when we tell them to someone else. Dreams we keep to ourselves can still help, and a dream that drifts back into the obscure reaches of our unconscious can still have a small effect on us during the day. But the effect is nothing compared to the festival of lights when that dream is remembered and then said out loud.

Chapter Summary

The history of dream interpretation in Western culture has led many of us to feel uncomfortable and inadequate when listening to dreams. The truth is there are only a few skills needed to listen to someone else's dreams. First, make it safe for your loved ones to share their dreams by telling them about your interest. Second, invite your loved ones to tell their dreams. Without an invitation, most people will assume their dreams still are not welcome. Finally, listen carefully without adding your own interpretation. Allow the dreamer to make sense of their own experience.

A dream's creative power comes most fully into being when we say the dream out loud. By putting words to our experience, we can hear more clearly the dream's central message, and how our dreaming mind connects with—reflects, encourages, amplifies, challenges—our waking days.

Talking about Dreams

- When was the last time someone told you about a dream?

- How can you invite your loved ones to tell their dreams?

- If you have children, what do they dream about most often? How often do you invite them to tell their dreams?

- How will you respond the next time someone asks you to interpret their dream for them?

Chapter Ten

How to Cultivate Your Dreams

The people in this book learned to lean on dreams when they most needed their solace and guidance. Dreams don't suddenly appear at the end of life, however. They walk with us throughout our lives, offering insight, humor, challenges, and comfort whenever we look for them. They can play as big a role in our daily life as they do at life's end, if we want and trust their help.

This chapter is designed to help you strengthen your waking connections with your dreams. You don't have to wait until the end of life to find the benefits this book describes. You can start now to build this trusting partnership with your dreams.

I can't guarantee you will have only sweet dreams from now on if you follow my suggestions. Bad dreams and awkward dreams and confusing dreams are all part of the dream package. What I can offer is a basic approach to dreams and dreaming that the people in this book have used. It can help you engage with your dreams and build a relationship you can trust between your waking and dreaming life.

This basic approach is not new. It has been used in other cultures around the world for centuries. Charles Laughlin counts approximately four thousand cultures, big and small, in the world today, and most of these other cultures engage with dreams as an ordinary aspect of daily life. Many recognize waking reality and dreaming reality as two distinct but equally valid ways of managing their lives. As a result, dreams play a more prominent role in their daily interactions.

In the cultures where dreams are considered integral to daily life, children are taught right from the beginning to pay attention to them. They are asked for their dreams daily and are expected to contribute to their community's well-being through their dreams. The community trusts all dreams can be helpful to the dreamer, the dreamer's family, or the larger community.

This trust in the ultimate usefulness of dreams encourages everyone to keep up the daily practice of telling dreams, even when occasional dreams appear convoluted or awkward. With this simple practice of paying attention, the dreamers invite dreams into a partnership. With regular practice dreams become more reliable and dependable in helping to solve problems and resolve interpersonal conflicts.

In modern Western culture we also go through intense training from early childhood on how to relate to our dreams, but with the opposite goal. We learn dreams are neither dependable nor reliable. We learn not to talk about dreams at school or work and to disregard the dreams of others as not real and therefore not trustworthy.

By the time we are adults, we have learned well how to let last night's images fall away almost before we open our eyes. We either forget or ignore nearly all of our dreams. As Laughlin writes, "These Western societies ... skew the development of consciousness away from [dreaming] and toward perceptual and cognitive processes oriented outward to the external world." [93] When we learn our first language, we quickly tune our ears to the sounds that hold meaning in our families and weed out any sounds they don't use to talk with us. In this same way we learn to weed out dream images because we are told early and often they mean nothing, can mean nothing.

For many people in Western culture, then, dreams are nothing more than a random scattering of images thrown together without regard for plot or story, and because they don't make much sense we have no reason to pay them much attention. We think these random scatterings prove everyone is right—that dreams are nonsensical—without realizing dreams need our help to become meaningful. Without our making sense of them, our next dreams feel as incomprehensible as a foreign language, which reinforces our belief that they can never be useful.

The good news is you can change this pattern without too much effort. Learning to engage with dreams is fairly straightforward and much easier than learning a new language. Our brains are already designed for dreams the same way they are designed for perception and memory. They churn out new

---

93. Laughlin, *Communing with the Gods,* 62–3. "Children are taught from infancy that dreams are not real ("It's just a dream, dear, go back to sleep"), and thus they just happen and can be ignored. Elementary schools typically do not address one's dream life, and information obtained in dreams, if any, bears little or no relevance to the waking world. Dreams, therefore, tend not to inform culture all that much, especially with respect to spiritual issues."

dreams every time we sleep, regardless of whether or not we remember them.

To find your dreams all you need to do is tell your brain to take note of them. You do that by telling yourself, "I want to remember my dreams." This is the first exercise and maybe the only exercise you will ever need. "I want to remember my dreams." Say it out loud or think it as you lie down to sleep, and see what happens. This is what people around the world have said to themselves, in one way or another, for thousands of years. "I want to remember my dreams."

This exercise may seem too simple to believe, but our brains really do work in concert with our wishes when it comes to remembering or noticing our environment. Our brains are wired to take in vast amounts of sensory input through our five senses, and then to filter out what is unimportant to us. Without conscious thought our brains distinguish the necessary information (that car is approaching too fast) from all the background noise in that moment (I smell exhaust, the car seat is warm, there are exactly eighteen cars within my direct line of sight at this moment, a red one, two blue ones, a pickup with one taillight out …). We don't have enough time to pay attention to detail, so our brains filter out of our conscious awareness some things, actually a lot of things. If we ever want to see more, we simply give our brains the instruction to pay attention.

Here is an example of how easily our conscious intention can direct what we see. Take a quick look around the room you are sitting in right now. What do you notice? Now close your eyes for a moment and tell yourself you want to notice the color blue. Think about all the different shades of blue and then open your eyes and look around again. You might be surprised at how quickly your brain now picks up different shades of blue in the room. The color was always there, but it was part of the room's background noise, an unimportant detail your brain filtered out. Once you tell yourself blue is important, your eyes will pick up the color almost effortlessly. Blue becomes ready to be noticed because of that one small request you made.

We can do the same with our dreams. We often treat dreams as so much background noise, something we push aside in favor of real life, and as a result the dreams become nearly invisible. When we tell ourselves that we want to remember our dreams, however, our brains will hold on to them long enough for us to notice, just as we noticed the color blue. Remember enough dreams and you begin to build a new neural pathway—a mental bridge between your waking and dreaming awareness.

Forge New Neural Pathways

According to Charles Laughlin, our preference for logic over and above intuition creates a wall between the two different functions—logic and intuition—in our brains. When we decide not to think about our dreams, we limit our rational thoughts to waking life concerns. This leaves our sleeping brain to rely almost solely on our creative, intuitive impulses for dreaming. As a result, what dreams we can remember seem fragmentary, illogical, fleeting, and scattered.

When you allow yourself to think about a dream while awake, you automatically activate your rational, logical brain to make sense out of the images you remember. This activation builds a new neural pathway—a bridge between your waking, rational mind and your sleeping, intuitive mind. The more often you consciously encourage your dream fragments to make sense, to become part of a coherent story, the more quickly your brain will do the same work in your dreams while you sleep. Over time your dreaming brain will begin to use logic and storytelling in the dreams. To you it will look like your dreams actually become more coherent and storylike. You will have more storylines (narratives) and fewer random images.

Your dreams also will become more clearly linked to your waking life concerns as your dreaming mind is influenced by your waking mind. You will encounter fewer outrageous monsters and more familiar adversaries. Your waking life will in turn feel more grounded, supported, and challenged by your dreams.

If you decide at some point you don't want to think about your dreams, the process happens in reverse. Stop thinking about dreams before bed and stop asking yourself to remember your dreams and the dreams will slide away. The neural pathways between your rational side and your intuitive side will fade from disuse, just as all skills eventually fade if we don't use them. Without access to that rational part of the brain, you will find your dreams once again becoming more scattered, erratic, and forgettable.

This is not a foolproof system. It takes practice and intention to develop these neural pathways, just as learning a new language or playing a new instrument or learning to drive takes time and intention. You will still wake up with dreams

that don't make sense, but you will find more of them connecting to your waking life. When you dream a fragmented
dream, you always retain the option to explore it further or
to let it go, trusting any important message will become clear
in a later dream.

Open a Conversation with Your Dreams

Remembering your dreams is a lot like having a conversation with a new friend. You open yourself to the unknown
of their opinions and thoughts and risk being surprised, delighted, irritated, or intrigued. You won't ever be in control
of the dream, just as you won't be in control of your friend's
thoughts and reactions. You won't always know what your
dreams will bring, just as you don't always know what your
friend will say, and that is how it should be.

As much as you learn about dreams in general, you will
never be in control of what dreams will come next. Not being in control and not knowing what will happen next are
two of the chief pleasures of dreaming. If you are willing to
listen, to open yourself to this unknown friend, you might
discover something intriguing (or disturbing or enlightening)
about yourself.

While I can influence how often I remember my dreams,
the dream images themselves are rarely under my conscious
control. My dreams surprise me, which I consider one of
their many strengths. I wake with unexpected images and
new insights. Sometimes my dreams frighten me, but more
often they delight me with their many threads connecting
my inner and outer lives.

If listening to dreams is like having a conversation with a trusted friend, then we already have all the tools we need to respond to them, based on the basic rules of etiquette. We can feel competent right away, even if the dreams themselves are still not making sense to us. There are three common-sense rules I follow for conversations with my friends that can also work for conversations with my dreams.

1. Invite dreams in.
2. Listen carefully.
3. Respond with respect.

These are the only three rules I know about most conversations, whether we are talking about the weather, recent car repairs, dreams, or our emotional and spiritual life. We invite conversation by asking questions and making it safe to answer. We clear our thoughts and feelings so we can listen well to what is being offered, and we respond with our best selves.

Invite Dreams In

When I was very young, my mother used to send me to bed with the phrase "Have good dreams." The message of kindness, warmth, and invitation became a routine and helped me look for good dreams as I lay my head down. Inviting dreams can be as simple as wishing your loved ones to have good dreams at night. Wishing good dreams to family and friends sets an expectation in everyone's mind that dreaming is a normal and often interesting part of sleep. Wishing good dreams reminds you and your loved ones that dreaming is allowed.

Some people call this setting an intention, meaning you consciously remind yourself that you want to remember good dreams. As you get ready to sleep each night, in the moment your head relaxes onto your pillow, think, "I want to remember my dreams." This tells your dreaming mind that you are interested and willing to remember whatever dreams come to you. You are also telling your rational Western mind to relax its guard against the supposed folly of dreams. You are creating a safe space within your memory for dream images to linger and asking your rational brain to make sense of them so they can be memorable.

Most dream rituals and habits, no matter how elaborate, have grown out of this basic tool of asking ourselves to remember our dreams. In ancient Western culture people traveled to distant temples created specifically for healing dreams. They were searching for big dreams—the dreams that could heal and transform their lives. They fasted and prayed to Asklepios, the god of healing, for important dreams. They wore special clothes, slept in specific rooms in the temple, and had their dreams interpreted by specially trained temple guardians.

In today's world, trips to the healing temples are rare events, but we sleep every night. We regularly give up conscious control of our body. We close our eyes and lay our heads down and wait patiently for sleep to overtake us, and we usually feel safe that we will awaken unharmed in a few hours' time. We have a regular sleep practice borne of physical necessity and of cultural habit, and in that habit we can add one small wish—for ourselves, for our loved ones—to have good dreams.

This approach to remembering dreams can be elaborated upon in any way that helps you remember. People who have a strong interest in their dreams often practice some modern adaptation of the ancient Greek ritual. They don't necessarily travel to distant lands, but they do find ways to make their good-dream wishes more specific. They might concentrate on a specific question they want answered before they go to sleep and ask for a dream to respond to that question. With more specific requests come more elaborate tasks to imprint the importance of their request on their sleeping mind. Some meditate on their question; some pray. Others set up record-ers and journals to show their intent to capture whatever dream images they remember the next morning.

Exactly from whom they are asking for these dreams re-mains entirely in their own hands. Some people will ask God or their guiding spirits for the dream. People in grief will ask their loved ones to come visit them. People who live too far away to be with their loved one might concentrate on trav-eling to them, to catch a glimpse of their loved one before their death. Artists look for the muse while scientists hope their extra focus will fire up their own creative problem-solving brain.

A friend of mine instructed her students to hold a glass of water in bed for five minutes before sleeping, concentrating on the question they want answered. In the morning they were to drink the water before getting out of bed and then write down whatever dream images came back to them. She taught them to ask the water for the dream, not because she thought water could answer them, but because she knew the water was a small ritual they could use to help concentrate their attention on what they want. Their focus on the water was to help them remember the dreams. They concentrate their attention and their desire for a dream over the water, and when they drink it the next morning they remind themselves again of their intention and desire.

Listen Carefully

The second requirement of building a relationship with your dreams is to pay attention to the dreams you remember. You have invited them in; now sit with them for a moment and listen. The act of listening to your dreams can also be as simple or as elaborate as you want to make it. The simplest approach is to give yourself a few minutes before you get out of bed to remember. Lie still for a few minutes, close your eyes again, and think about the images and feelings floating through your head. Some people will wake with entire movies running through their brains, adventures in unfamiliar landscapes, people they love, and random strangers, and their stories will wind through five or six scenes. Others will wake with a single image.

Remembering your dreams well enough to hear their messages takes practice and patience with yourself. At first you might not remember much more than fragments of conversation, a color or song snippet, and you will question whether or not the new dream is worth the trouble of developing this habit. Try living with your dream for part of your day. If you can't remember anything but a line from a song, see how much of the song you can remember. Hum it in the shower and think about what the song reminds you of.

Listening to dreams is not about analyzing them. Listening is about paying attention, either to their details or to how they are affecting you. You can ask the same straightforward questions of your dreams as the people in this book have asked: What happened and how did you feel? What does it remind you of? As the Reverend Dr. Jeremy Taylor, dream expert and author, is fond of saying, our dreams belong to us, come to us for our benefit, and will speak to us in a language we can understand.

Many dreams use images and events from our daily lives. As you begin to recognize these inspirations for your dreams, you will find dreams are perhaps less mysterious and more closely attuned to your waking needs than you might have thought. You will find a new reason to trust your dreams are working in partnership with you.

My friend Patricia is a psychologist who studied Jung's work in graduate school, but her favorite way of holding a particularly vivid dream is to imagine she is carrying it around with her through her day. Patricia calls it "walking with her dream." When she remembers a dream she wants to explore, she imagines carefully tucking the dream into her pocket, close at hand so she can look at her day from the perspective of the dream. She asks what is different about the world now that she has had this dream? How does her day look with this dream now in her life? What does it make her think about now that she had this dream? She listens to the dream by looking at her waking life through the lens of its images. She allows the dream enough room to breathe into her day.

I love this idea of walking around with my dreams, and I have tried it a number of times. Once I dreamed I was flying through the clouds—no plane, it was just me whizzing across the globe, free and gleeful—and I woke up feeling elated by the experience. And even though I had no other reason for elation, I carried that joy of flight with me through the day. I allowed my mood to be influenced by the dream because what could be better than remembering the exhilaration of flight as I walked along the street? I allowed the emotional energy of my dream to permeate the barrier between my sleeping and waking mind and influence the emotional tone of my day.

If you can hold on to the emotions of your dreams during your waking life, you will add to the neural pathway Laughlin describes. This will make it that much easier to take your waking, logical self back into your dreams and bring a story-like order to the more random images.

You can put your dreams into logical order by giving them a title or headline, like "This is the one where I stood in line for hours, I don't know why" or "This is the one where I was falling and woke up before I landed." These are not titles of great literature, but using an easy shorthand title helps you recognize and amplify the dream's message. It highlights the dream's meaning to you, even if that meaning sometimes doesn't reach beyond "I don't know." The meaning you find will in turn help you remember the details that support this meaning, which teaches your dreaming brain that you want stories.

You can think about the actions and decisions you made in the dream. Ask yourself if you would make those same decisions in your waking life and what you might have done differently if you had been more aware it was a dream. In this way you begin to respond to your dreams.

Respond with Respect

Conversations of all kinds require a back-and-forth exchange. If one person does all the talking without any feedback or response from the other person, the conversation ends or perhaps wasn't a real conversation in the first place. In respectful conversations I respond to what is being said. I allow what is said to affect me in some way. Responding with respect doesn't mean I agree with everything I hear. I may argue or laugh or applaud or launch into another story to build on what my friend is saying. Responding with respect means I respect the person who is speaking. I respect the right of the other person to speak his or her mind.

The same can be said for how we interact with our dreams. Any response, whether we have planned it carefully or reacted without thought, will influence the content and frequency of the next dream. Through our responses, we are training our dreams in what we want most to hear next, what we can tolerate in terms of images, and what stories carry the strongest and clearest emotional messages.

To build a trusting relationship with my dreams I need to respond to them with the same respect I would give to a new friend. I don't give up my right to disagree or laugh or change the subject, just as with any conversation, but if I wish to remain in a relationship with my dreams, I need to accord them the same right to be heard that I give all my friends.

The range of what makes a response respectful can vary as widely as the dreamers who remember them. Paying attention to your dream will by itself encourage your brain to remember more dreams in the future, which is a type of simple response. Beyond that, you can audio record your dreams, write them down in a journal, tell someone, or talk them out in the shower. Some people have created mobile apps and websites to help people record and categorize their dream images. These are all ways to listen more deeply to a dream without acting on its particular message.

Other people are more comfortable doing something active in response to the dream. For some this means following a dream's impulse the next morning. Some people create art, music, or poetry to express their dreams. Some people find solutions to problems that had been bothering them and then put them into action the following day. Scientists dream about their work as often as artists, and some have followed their dreams to scientific breakthroughs.

Dream groups and therapist offices offer insightful, indepth dream work that is helpful for those who want to put in that kind of time and effort, but such intense concentration is not necessary to build a trusting relationship with our dreams.

Responding to a dream means respecting that it has something to say, regardless of whether or not you agree with it. You can question your dreams, challenge their logic, and evaluate them for their sheer pragmatic usefulness. You can allow the images to deepen your spiritual journey, finding in them answers to prayers and glimpses of another world.

Use the dream as a starting point in your conversation instead of wishing (or fearing) the dream holds all the answers to your life. Ask yourself, what did you like about the dream? What did it remind you of? What would you do or say differently if you were to dream it again? You can reimagine the dreams you don't like and add your own ending, just as we re-imagine conversations that didn't go well the first time.

Dream Appreciation for Beginners

The kind of dream appreciation I've been discussing in this book—*What did you dream? How do you feel? What does it remind you of?*—is a basic dream interpretation. Easy to remember and comforting in the way it builds a bridge between waking and dreaming life, it helps dreamers feel competent with their dreams right away. There is nothing wrong with the more complex dream work that some people pursue, but that level of attention is not necessary in order to build a trusting partnership with your dreams.

Using the basic dream appreciation approach in this book is often enough for me. It gives me enough insight that I can feel I am in partnership with my dreams. The dreams become one doorway into understanding how I am managing my life right now. I stay with the dream long enough to see what it points to, but I don't worry about what the dream may be hiding. I don't pay much attention to mythic symbols, allegories, or literary illusions that might lurk beneath the surface. I am sure my dreams use these metaphors, but I know I don't have to take the time to explore them before I feel satisfied with the dream's message.

This dream appreciation is a lot like learning basic cooking skills. The end results are not as fancy, and most would agree it doesn't produce as complex a blend of flavors in the final tasting. Basic cooking, however, is satisfying, nutritious, and easy to do on a busy schedule. It gets the job done, and it can be fun and engaging without taking too much effort.

It allows the cook's attention to wander back into other important parts of life.

Learning basic cooking skills can help anyone feel competent as they meet the obligation to take care of themselves. For aspiring chefs these basic skills form the foundation in a life of culinary exploration, but for many people basic skills are all the tools they will use in life, and their cooking feels like home and comfort to the people who love them.

This basic dream appreciation may pique your interest in a life of in-depth dream exploration, or it can sustain you through the rest of your life just as it is. Children, young adults, elders, people who are sick, and people who have been healthy all their lives have all found benefit in asking themselves these few foundational questions: What happened in the dream? How did I feel? What does it remind me of now?

The questions begin a conversation with dreams that remains simple and direct. I have been delighted to see how many dream experts encourage their readers to take their dreams into their own hands. As Bulkeley and Bulkley write in *Dreaming Beyond Death:*

> We really want to emphasize this: *You can understand your own dreams.* All humans are natural dreamers, and all of us have the inherent capacity to make sense of our dreams and learn valuable lessons from them. Each of us is our own best expert when it comes to discerning their meanings.[94]

All you need now is trust.

---

94. Bulkeley and Bulkley, *Dreaming Beyond Death*, 135.

Trust Your Dreams, Trust Yourself

All dream interpretation comes down to a question of trust. Not just whether we trust the dream can be beneficial, but whether we trust ourselves to make good sense of what we dream. In modern Western culture we have been taught not only to distrust dreams because they are nonsense, but also to distrust our own ability to make sense of our dreams.

When Freud and Jung showed how important dreams could be, they also developed elaborate rules of interpretation and, as a result, nonprofessionals came to believe they are not competent to assess their own dreams for themselves. Too many people have given up their right to interpret their own dreams. This is a genuine loss. I might not understand my dreams as completely as someone else, but they are still my dreams, pushing forward with the express purpose of making my life better, and I have the right to make my own best sense of them.

A middle-aged man told me the other day that he had falling dreams that only ended when he hit the ground and was jolted awake. The dreams felt vivid and frightening, and they confused him. Why should he dream of falling so often? What does it mean that he wakes so frightened? He searched the Internet and found several explanations that didn't seem to fit him. Over the past centuries people have built up an impressive array of potential meanings for falling dreams, including stress, fear of failing, fear of success, feeling out of control in daily life, relationship issues, health issues—the list is endless.

The problem for this man was that he had thought he was having a pretty good life. He wasn't particularly stressed or feeling out of control, and he wasn't having a fear of failure as far as he could tell. Either the meanings weren't fitting his life or he was having unconscious fears and *now* what was he supposed to do? He wondered if he should get counseling help to explore a potential hidden anxiety.

This man could explore the psychological ramifications of falling with a therapist, of course, but he could also find a new way to engage with the dream. I asked him what it felt like to hit the ground, and he said, "I am always terrified, but I don't wake up until I actually hit." I asked him why not wake up earlier, and he snorted. "I don't back down from a fight." He sounded so proud that it got the two of us talking about courage and what it takes to allow oneself to actually hit the ground in a falling dream. He was surprised to learn most people who have this common falling dream jerk awake before hitting the ground. Soon, he was talking about the adrenaline rush he gets in waking life when taking a risk.

Within just a few minutes he had moved from fearing his dream was showing him some secret unconscious unhappiness to feeling proud of his courage. For the first time he saw his courage alongside the terror within his dream and could see his willingness to face the end of his fall as a choice he was making despite his fear. His dream became less a message of inner torment and more a reminder of his personal courage, something he valued highly. I suggested next time he found himself falling he could try turning it into a flying dream, like an airplane's touch-and-go, and his eyes lit up.

"I can do that?" he asked. "Where would I go?"

"Anywhere you want," I answered and smiled at him.

That ten-minute conversation, as short as it was, helped him feel better equipped for his next falling dream. Could his dream have deeper psychological layers to it? Yes, of course. His dream could mean any of those things, and he might at some point find one of those meanings helpful in exploring his waking life. But they weren't helping him now.

When this man connected his dream to his daily life, he found his courage and a way to imaginatively change his role in the dream from a helpless victim to an active participant. His dreams gave him a way to experience both his courage and his fear in a genuine exchange of feelings and ideas. An in-depth dream analysis wouldn't have hurt, to be sure, but it wasn't necessary for him to feel back in control of his life and of a dream that had bothered him. Both of these responses are acceptable, and both could help him.

Any response that treats the dream as if it has the right to be remembered is a respectful response. You don't have to always understand what the dream images mean. If the dreams you remember don't make sense, you can let them go and try again another day. Just don't give up. If you want to get better at dreaming, you will need to trust that your dreams ultimately come to help you, just as you will ultimately be the one to make sense of them.

Like all good friends, your dreams will talk to you in a language you can understand. You will find that, just like in the best conversations with friends, your dreams will respond to your interests and your requests. The more attention you give to your dreams, the more vibrant, coherent, introspective, and all-around more interesting they will become. Like the best of friendships, dreams will at times invite you to think and feel more deeply about your life and your relationships. You won't be in conscious control of what images they show you, but you always have a say in the conversation, and your dreams will be influenced by how you respond to them. You still decide what you think and feel and how you will respond. Your dreams are here for you, and they are yours.

Dreams are at once both unfettered from the daily conventions of time and space and deeply attached to your personal waking life. They serve you by showing you your own deepest fears and greatest hopes. They bring new insights and sweet escapes and terrors to overcome, all to help you grow as a human being. They are always, always loyal to your interests.

Chapter Summary

In dreams we allow ourselves to loosen our grip on the limitations of physical reality. We explore other perspectives on waking life, solve problems, use our dream images to make new connections, and create a new story for our life.

To naturally strengthen your waking relationship with your dreams, you need take only a few simple steps. First, tell yourself you want to remember your dreams. Then, when you do remember a dream, take a few minutes to make your own sense of what it means. Finally, respond to your dream as if it is worthy of your attention.

Trust your dreams are here to help you even if you don't like or understand some of the images you remember. Even bad dreams can help us manage our lives better by illuminating our worries. Trust yourself that you can handle the wide range of emotions your dreams may bring. You can always wake up and leave the dream if you need to, and you can always go back and change the script later.

Trust you can find your own balance between waking and dreaming, a balance that fits your life and allows you to lean on your dreams as you see fit. You are allowed to make sense of your dreams in any way that feels right to you. And when you and your family face the next crisis of a life ending, whether it be your own or that of someone you love, your dream practice will make it that much easier for your dreams to help support you all.

Talking about Dreams

- Do you trust your dreams exist to help you in your daily life? Why or why not?

- What connection have you found between your dreams and your spiritual beliefs? Do your dreams help you deepen your faith or do they challenge what you know? Why do you think your dreams do this?

- What connections have you found between your dreams and your waking life? Do your dreams reflect or respond to your waking life, bring only random images, or take you on unfamiliar adventures? Why do you think your dreams do this?

Epilogue:
Dreams of Purpose and Meaning

In the introduction I wrote that dreams can help us on three different levels at the end of life, and I have tried to touch on all those levels throughout the book. The first level is their content. Dreams bring us images, stories, and messages that speak directly to our lives. The images bring comfort, sometimes challenge us, and give us another way to think about what we want and who we are. The second level of help comes when we talk about our dreams with people we trust. By telling our dreams we offer the gift of revealing our inner lives to people we love. A dream that is shared can bring families together and help us begin the difficult but important conversations we need to have with each other. Telling our dreams makes them more brilliant and helps us find new depths of meaning and spirituality in them.

The third level is our dreaming mind's assumption that what we feel and think still matters, that we still matter, and that we are not done living. This understanding is not so well defined as a concrete dream image or action, and as a consequence it is less easily shared out loud with others. In fact, none of the people I interviewed for this book mentioned this understanding to me. But the dream's firm conviction that the dreamer's life remains one of meaning and purpose adds a strong voice for dignity at a time when dignity is often in doubt.

As much as this book has been about dreams and their healing potential, it has also been anchored in the bewildering pain of dying, death, and grief. As people approach the end of life, they often are forced by their waning strength to confront the question of what makes their life worth living.

An elderly woman who was fast losing her ability to care for herself once said to me, "I won't be good for anything anymore. I don't know why I'm still here. I might as well be dead and get this over with." Not surprisingly, her family vehemently disagreed with her. Her daughter asked me, "Doesn't she realize how much I would do for her to have her stay with me one more day? Doesn't she know she is my mom? She's the only person who can ever love me as my mother, the only one who can smile at me with her eyes?"

This woman, like many people I've met, did know her family loved her. What she wasn't so sure about was whether she was still worthy of their love. She could no longer see any way in which she contributed to her family, something that had carried her purpose in life. She saw the increasing amount of care she needed as too great for the little bit she could still offer them in return.

The end of life raises the eternal human questions. Is my life meaningful? Can I hold on to my dignity in the midst of physical dependence? Is my life worth the burden of care I will need? Why should I linger in this limbo, not fully alive but not yet dead? Why not be done already?

What brings a sense of purpose and meaning to most of us in the middle of life—work, productivity, family responsibilities—often falls away as our bodies become frail and dependent. When we can no longer move freely in the world and the burden of caring for us grows, we need to know why we are still living. We need to know we can offer something of worth to our families and friends. When that usefulness is no longer readily apparent, we wonder why we should accept becoming a burden on those we once protected and supported.

Researchers are finding the less purpose and meaning people feel in their lives, the less self-worth they feel and the more they fret about how much physical care they might eventually need at the end of their lives. In countries and states where assistance in dying is legal, studies are showing that somewhere between 58 percent and 95 percent of the people who do end their lives early cite their fear of being a burden as their primary reason.[95] What makes this information more heartbreaking is that feeling like a burden often doesn't match how much care people actually required. Instead, the fear of being a burden matched most closely with their lack of self-worth, dignity, purpose, and meaning.

The hard truth is most of us will have to live through some period of time, whether days or months or years, when we will need care from others. Barring accidents, acts of violence,

---

95. Keith G. Wilson, Dorothyann Curran, and Christine J. McPherson, "A Burden to Others: A Common Source of Distress for the Terminally Ill," *Cognitive Behaviour Therapy* 34 (2005): 115–123. doi:10.1080/16506070510008461.

or sudden medical catastrophes, most of us will experience some form of dependency, at least for a while.

This hasn't always been true. For thousands of years most human illnesses were sudden and final. Few people lingered in a state of prolonged debility. They took sick and died, often at home, often within a week or two from such medical crises as infections, accidents, childhood illness, and childbirth. As medicine improved people began surviving these acute crises. We lived longer, long enough to die of illnesses that moved more slowly, like heart disease and cancer.

The practice of medicine also changed with the lengthening of life. For decades doctors felt morally obligated to keep the harsh news of fatal diagnoses hidden from the people who were ill. As a standard of care, they hid the worst diagnoses from their patients and instead told patients they were getting better. Doctors often told the families that their loved one was dying, but then encouraged the families to keep the secret. Doctors treated the fact of a person's dying as potentially emotionally devastating news.

Doctors protected their patients from the truth of their illness in large part because no one believed a rational human being would put up with living through a prolonged fatal illness. Their goal was to give the dying person as many good days as they could possibly have, free from the emotional suffering that comes with the knowledge that death is near. They hid the truth out of kindness, to foster hope, to provide days of respite, and to help people live as fully as possible. In many ways, they feared the very conversation the woman at the beginning of this chapter began with me.

As long as no one asked dying people what they knew or thought, families could believe their dying loved one was living in blissful ignorance, enjoying their last days free from care and talking about the future as if it remained open. It was all a lie, but for many it seemed like a necessary lie.

Elizabeth Kübler-Ross was the first to ask the people she knew were dying what they thought about their futures. In 1969 she published her groundbreaking book, *On Death and Dying,* in which she revealed that not only did dying people know they were dying, but they often felt obligated to pretend they felt fine in order to protect their families and doctors. For the sake of the people they loved, they pretended to be getting better, pretended to enjoy their good health, all the while feeling frightened and miserable and emotionally isolated, unable to speak the truth of their lives. Everyone suffered.

Kübler-Ross's work ushered in a change in how medicine was practiced and how we approach the end of someone's life. Medical professionals gradually let go of their insistence on protecting patients from the terrible truth and began to acknowledge their patients' rights to make their own informed choices in health care, including their right to know when the end of life approached.

Now most of us can expect to be told when treatments are no longer working. Now, more than at any other time in the history of the world, most of us can expect to live through a period of time in which we know our life is short but not yet over. We are moving as a group into an emotional landscape that has few precedents. Living with the end of life means living with a future we know is limited, one that will be filled with multiple losses and dwindling energy reserves.

We will have to learn how to live well with the near presence of death in a way few before us ever considered. We will have to decide anew what makes a good life and how we will honor the inner life of thinking and feeling, wondering and loving, as our physical strength dwindles away. Right now we have few words or models to guide us through such a passage, but I am hopeful that at some point in the near future, the end of life will come to be seen as a new stage of human growth and development every bit as important and challenging as childhood, adolescence, and middle age.

At the end of life our need for meaning, purpose, self-worth, and dignity doesn't fade away; these four values remain deeply entangled within our hearts. If anything these values grow stronger. This is precisely the moment when dreams offer their greatest gift. Remembering the occasional dream won't fix our lives or give us more days, but a dream can offer each of us a reconnection to our life's deepest meaning and purpose, however we choose to define it. Quietly and insistently, our dreams reaffirm that who we are matters and what we feel and think remains important and worthwhile. Dreams build on the unwavering assumption that we are not yet done offering ourselves to the world.

No matter what the dream images show, they come with the purpose of helping us better understand ourselves, as if understanding ourselves remains an essential goal right up to the last day of life. Dreams remind us of how our lives fit together. Some dreams help us review our life choices and show us again how we became who we are. Some dreams remind us of what we still need to do or what we want to give our loved ones. When dreams challenge us, they help us better understand how we are living and what choices are left for us to make. When we respond to our dreams by telling them out loud or just thinking about them, we let ourselves be reminded of who we are in our soul and what we most want in the time we have left. Through our dreams our emotional lives become important for the sole reason that we are important.

In a way, each of our dreams becomes a kind of Greek chorus—the nameless characters that stand to one side of the drama and comment about the action on stage. Like a Greek chorus, our dreams comment on our daily life, lending us new depth and perspective. They echo our strongest emotions and underline the main lessons we are trying to learn. They warn and scold and celebrate with us, and they remind us of our deepest values. They add weight and power to moments that might otherwise have slipped by unremarked. Our dreams don't seem to care how many minutes or days we have left. In dreams each day holds an unlimited present moment in which we can choose again how we want to live. Dreams push us to understand more, gather another insight, give another loving gaze, and offer another moment of grace to those around us. We have work to do that will make a difference, right up until our end.

In the first pages of this book, a man who had less than a week to live woke from a dream about his former wife that changed his life. It helped him resolve a conflicted relationship with his wife, who was herself long-since deceased. Someone observing this dream and resolution from a distance might wonder what had been the point? Sure, he found again his deep appreciation for a woman he had once loved, but he died only a few days later. What did it matter what he felt anymore?

By dreaming of his wife, this man discovered he wasn't just waiting to die. His dream told him it mattered what he felt and that his memories and relationship were as important now as they had ever been. Without ever saying it out loud, his dream made the fundamental assertion that his life in these last few days had purpose.

When he told the dream to his daughter, she was changed as well. She was given the gift of witnessing her parents reconcile, even if only in this dream. She saw her father relax into a calm peace, which brought her relief. It opened her to the possibility of an afterlife in a new way as she wondered along with her father if he would see his wife again. Now, several years later, her father's last dream has become part of this family's memory of his whole life.

Dreams insist our lives have purpose and then they leave it to us to find that purpose. By finding what a dream means to us, to what and to whom it connects us, we allow the fire of the dream to relight and illuminate a fuller waking life. We are not just waiting until our hearts stop beating. Dreams help us reweave our past and present into a new understanding of life.

I have listened to many people go over the significant choices they made and how those choices shaped their lives— decisions to marry this person and not that one, have two children but not three, go back to school, follow an old dream into a new life. Whether we look back through memory or through a dream, we have another chance to see how our choices led to this moment. The end of life becomes one part of a much greater story that arcs through an entire life. Nothing is wasted; no decision is meaningless; no feeling is useless.

The people in this book have used dreams to open much-needed conversations with their loved ones. Some have delighted in dreams that gave them respite from the pains of their illness. They have leaned on dreams for comfort and hope and shared their dreams in a way that held their families through their own grief.

Dreams at the end of life bring to light whatever the dreamer needs, whether it be asking spiritual questions, remembering mundane tasks, or revisiting past troubling events. Each dream remains dedicated to the dreamer's well-being. Dreams can help us keep our emotional and spiritual balance through the hardest days imaginable. Our dreams help us build emotional connections with those we love, and occasionally a dream will give us a glimpse of a reality that transcends daily life. Through dreams we find a new place waiting for us, whether we know this place resides within a spiritual realm or within the beauty of the earth. Dreams give us hope for what lies beyond physical death.

More than anything else, dreams remind each dreamer that we are still alive, still not done, and still able to provide a final gift to our families. The process of telling dreams restores a missing balance between the care we need and what we can still contribute to the life of our family. Dreams rest on the assumption that what we feel and think about our life is still important because we are important and because our thoughts and feelings matter to us and to the people who love us. This alone brings a healing that nothing else can approach.

Dreams at the end of life remind us of our inner strengths, our spiritual beliefs, and our most personal goals. They help us deepen our emotional bonds with the people we love. They gently lead us back, over and over, to the wonder of our hearts.

Reprinted Materials

The following previously published materials have been granted permission for use in *Dreams at the Threshold*:

To Write to the Author

If you wish to contact the author or would like more information about this book, please write to the author in care of Llewellyn Worldwide Ltd. and we will forward your request. Both the author and publisher appreciate hearing from you and learning of your enjoyment of this book and how it has helped you. Llewellyn Worldwide Ltd. cannot guarantee that every letter written to the author can be answered, but all will be forwarded. Please write to:

Jeanne Van Bronkhorst
℅ Llewellyn Worldwide
2143 Wooddale Drive
Woodbury, MN 55125-2989

Please enclose a self-addressed stamped envelope for reply, or $1.00 to cover costs. If outside the U.S.A., enclose an international postal reply coupon.

Premonitions
in
Daily Life

Working with
Spontaneous Information
when Rational Understanding
Fails You

JEANNE VAN BRONKHORST

Premonitions in Daily Life
Working with Spontaneous Information
When Rational Understanding Fails You
Jeanne Van Bronkhorst

While the generally accepted definition of premonitions involves dark warnings or visions of terrible events to come, the truth is most premonitions are about the ordinary moments in daily life. They can occur in a variety of ways, from sudden and intense apprehension to the subtle whisper of intuition.

Premonitions in Daily Life is the only book that investigates the deeper meanings behind premonitions. Most similar titles begin and end with the question of whether or not they exist, and never explore the important concerns: What do premonitions say about me? How do I respond? How do I make sense of premonitions when my culture doesn't believe in them?

This in-depth, three-part guide shows how to identify premonitions in your life, demystifies the assumptions and fears about them, and thoroughly demonstrates how to respond with common sense and without challenging your beliefs.

978-0-7387-3475-0, 288 pp., 6 x 9   **$14.99**

To order, call 1-877-NEW-WRLD
Prices subject to change without notice
Order at Llewellyn.com 24 hours a day, 7 days a week!

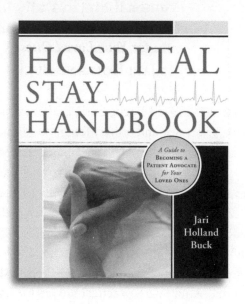

HOSPITAL
STAY
HANDBOOK

A Guide to
Becoming a
Patient Advocate
for Your
Loved Ones

Jari
Holland
Buck

Hospital Stay Handbook
A Guide to Becoming a Patient Advocate for Your Loved Ones
Jari Holland Buck

When Jari Holland Buck's husband became seriously ill, she stayed by his side and bravely fought for his life. Her steadfast attention to detail-questioning caregivers, researching medicines, and providing a positive, spiritually rich environment for healing produced a medical miracle: his survival.

The author's vivid experiences form the basis of this guide to becoming a patient advocate. Her life-saving lessons will help you choose the best hospital, develop a partnership with caregivers, prevent medical mistakes, and avoid caregiver burnout. Along with practical advice for enforcing patient rights, executing power of attorney, and avoiding inappropriate hospital charges, the author also explores how to bolster the body, mind, and soul of a critically ill loved one through prayer, positivity, and spiritual healing.

978-0-7387-1224-6, 264 pp., 7½ x 9⅛   **$18.95**